WORDSWORTH
& HIS POETRY

WORDSWORTH
& HIS POETRY

BY

WILLIAM HENRY HUDSON

KENNIKAT PRESS
Port Washington, N. Y./London

WORDSWORTH & HIS POETRY

First published in 1914
Reissued in 1970 by Kennikat Press
Library of Congress Catalog Card No: 70-103193
SBN 8046-0830-X

Manufactured by Taylor Publishing Company   Dallas, Texas

GENERAL PREFACE

A GLANCE through the pages of this little book will suffice to disclose the general plan of the series of which it forms a part. Only a few words of explanation, therefore, will be necessary.

The point of departure is the undeniable fact that with the vast majority of young students of literature a living interest in the work of any poet can best be aroused, and an intelligent appreciation of it secured, when it is immediately associated with the character and career of the poet himself. The cases are indeed few and far between in which much fresh light will not be thrown upon a poem by some knowledge of the personality of the writer, while it will often be found that the most direct—perhaps even the only—way to the heart of its meaning lies through a consideration of the circumstances in which it had its birth. The purely æsthetic critic may possibly object that a poem should be regarded simply as a self-contained and detached piece of art, having no personal affiliations or bearings. Of the validity of this as an abstract principle nothing need now be said. The fact remains that, in the earlier stages of study at any rate, poetry is most valued and loved when it is made to seem most human and vital ; and the human and vital interest of poetry can be most surely brought home to the reader by the biographical method of interpretation.

5

GENERAL PREFACE

This is to some extent recognized by writers of histories and text-books of literature, and by editors of selections from the works of our poets ; for place is always given by them to a certain amount of biographical material. But in the histories and text-books the biography of a given writer stands by itself, and his work has to be sought elsewhere, the student being left to make the connexion for himself ; while even in our current editions of selections there is little systematic attempt to link biography, step by step, with production.

This brings us at once to the chief purpose of the present series. In this, biography and production will be considered together and in intimate association. In other words, an endeavour will be made to interest the reader in the lives and personalities of the poets dealt with, and at the same time to use biography as an introduction and key to their writings.

Each volume will therefore contain the life-story of the poet who forms its subject. In this, attention will be specially directed to his personality as it expressed itself in his poetry, and to the influences and conditions which counted most as formative factors in the growth of his genius. This biographical study will be used as a setting for a selection, as large as space will permit, of his representative poems. Such poems, where possible, will be reproduced in full, and care will be taken to bring out their connexion with his character, his circumstances, and the movement of his mind. Then, in

GENERAL PREFACE

addition, so much more general literary criticism will be incorporated as may seem to be needed to supplement the biographical material, and to exhibit both the essential qualities and the historical importance of his work.

It is believed that the plan thus pursued is substantially in the nature of a new departure, and that the volumes of this series, constituting as they will an introduction to the study of some of our greatest poets, will be found useful to teachers and students of literature, and no less to the general lover of English poetry.

WILLIAM HENRY HUDSON

POEMS QUOTED IN WHOLE

SONNETS

POEMS QUOTED IN PART

WORDSWORTH
& HIS POETRY

THE life of Wordsworth yields little of interest to the biographer in search of materials for a good story. It was a long life of continuous industry and of great achievement. But so far as outward fortunes were concerned it was singularly uneventful. Some stir of excitement, it is true, entered into it during a few years of storm and stress. That excitement, however, was over by the time Wordsworth was twenty-six, and with his settlement at Grasmere, when he had still half a century of poetic activity before him, "the external events of his life," to use the words of one of his most sympathetic critics, "may be said to come to an end." Henceforth he dwelt for the most part in retirement and "from the crowded street remote "[1]; not indeed as a recluse, for he was never that; but as one who, like Cowper, looked out upon the world by preference "through the loopholes of retreat." It was a happy life, too—and happy lives are notoriously undramatic; a life of steady calm, broken only by those occasional sorrows which are inseparable from the common human lot. Even the interest of struggle against circumstance was lacking in it. For many years Wordsworth was poor. But he never had to fight his way. To one of his frugal habits the

"The Excursion," 1.

11

meagre resources of his early manhood were ample for all immediate needs ; and as fresh needs arose a kindly providence seemed ever ready to meet them.

Nor must we expect to find in Wordsworth's biography much of that inner interest which in the life of a man of letters often takes the place of the outer interest which we look for in the life of a man of action. His intellectual history after manhood had been reached was almost as uneventful as the history of his external career. At thirty his mind had come to its full development, and he had learned from experience all that experience had to teach. Then his thought hardened, and the hardening process inevitably meant cessation of growth. His own refusal to admit a chronological arrangement of his poems, perverse as it certainly was, had therefore this amount of justification, that such an arrangement would have little to tell us about the evolution of his mind.

> My heart leaps up when I behold
> A rainbow in the sky :
> So was it when my life began ;
> So is it now I am a man ;
> So be it when I shall grow old,
>   Or let me die !
> The Child is father of the Man ;
> And I could wish my days to be
> Bound each to each by natural piety.

These familiar lines deserve to be placed where Wordsworth placed them, in the forefront of his collective works, for they express not only, as he intended, the continuity, but also the striking uniformity of his intellectual life.

Though, as we shall see, the connexion between Wordsworth's poetry and his personal experience is of the closest kind, a comparatively slight body of narrative will therefore serve us here as the framework of our study. It will, moreover, be clear that in the writing of this narrative the demands of symmetry must be disregarded, since for our purposes a much fuller treatment is required of the years in which his character was being formed and the lines of his work determined, than of that long after-period during which, his poetic education complete and his plans fully settled,[1] his mind rested at peace within itself. It is fortunate that in what is thus the most important part of our subject we shall be able to rely upon the authority of the poet himself. When on his retirement to "his native mountains" he resolved "to construct a literary work that might live," it was, he felt, "a reasonable thing " that before addressing himself to his task " he should take a review of his own mind, and examine how far Nature and Education had qualified him for such an employment." He therefore "undertook to record, in verse, the origin and progress of his own powers, as far as he was acquainted with them"[2]; and the result was the long autobiographical poem

---

[1] See "The Prelude," xiv. 302-311.   [2] Preface to "The Excursion."

which, kept in manuscript till after his death, was then published under the title suggested by his widow—" The Prelude." Wordsworth regarded it as a " thing unprecedented in literary history that a man should talk so much about himself," [1] and he very justly found fault with its " redundancies." Yet its wealth of minute detail makes it specially valuable, and if in many places it is prolix and even dull, it is always illuminating. This poem we shall here take as our chief guide through the first thirty years of Wordsworth's life, drawing upon it freely even when its actual language is not reproduced.

II

WILLIAM WORDSWORTH was born on April 7, 1770, at Cockermouth, Cumberland. His father, John Wordsworth, was an attorney-at-law and land-agent to Sir James Lowther, afterwards Lord Lonsdale ; his mother Anne (Cookson), the daughter of a flourishing Penrith tradesman. He was the second of five children, his elder brother Richard being his senior by two years. Then came the one girl of the family, Dorothy, whose name is indissolubly linked with his own, and the two younger brothers, John and Christopher.

William was only eight when a great calamity

[1] Letter to Beaumont, May 1, 1805. Evidently he forgot Montaigne and Rousseau.

befell the family in the death of his " honoured mother " :

> she who was the heart
> And hinge of all our learnings and our loves :
> She left us destitute, and, as we might,
> Trooping together.[1]

His wife's premature death was a blow from which John Wordsworth never recovered, and he himself followed her six years later at the early age of forty-two.   William, then fourteen, was at that time a schoolboy at Hawkshead, Lancashire.

The venerable Grammar School at Hawkshead was then one of the best educational establishments in the north of England, and Wordsworth's recollections of his nine years there (1778–1787) were entirely pleasant.   The boys did not live in dormitories, but boarded out with " dames " in and about the " antique market-village." [2]   This feature of school life kept a special place in his memory.

> Ye lowly cottages wherein we dwelt,
> A ministration of your own was yours ;
> Can I forget you, being as you were
> So beautiful among the pleasant fields
> In which ye stood ? or can I here forget
> The plain and seemly countenance with which
> Ye dealt out your plain comforts ? [3]

He recalled with particular satisfaction the " home-amusements by the warm peat fire "

---

[1] " The Prelude," v. 157–260.   [2] " The Excursion," i. 53.
[3] " The Prelude," i. 499–505.

WORDSWORTH & HIS POETRY

in the long winter evenings, and the games of
whist and loo and other pastimes " too humble
to be named in verse," while outside " incessant
rain was falling, or the frost raged bitterly " ;
and if the " daily meals were frugal," they were
wholesome and were seasoned with " vigorous
hunger."   His own dame during his whole
school-time was an elderly spinster named Anne
Tyson, a warm-hearted, motherly creature of
whom afterwards he always spoke in terms of
great affection.   How deep was the hold Hawkshead had gained upon him is shown by the fact
that as soon as the first summer vacation
released him from Cambridge, he hastened back
thither, saw again with delight

>   the snow-white church upon her hill
> Sit like a thronèd Lady, sending out
> A gracious look all over her domain,[1]

and " with eager footsteps " reached " the
cottage threshold " which was the special object
of his pilgrimage.   Then followed all the
pleasures which attend the renewing of old
associations.

> Glad welcome had I, with some tears, perhaps,
> From my old Dame, so kind and motherly,
> While she perused me with a parent's pride.
> The thoughts of gratitude shall fall like dew
> Upon thy grave, good creature !   While my heart
> Can beat never will I forget thy name.
> Heaven's blessing be upon thee where thou liest
> After thy innocent and busy stir

[1] "The Prelude," iv. 21-23.

16

In narrow cares, thy little daily growth
Of calm enjoyments, after eighty years,
And more than eighty, of untroubled life ;
Childless, yet by the strangers to thy blood
Honoured with little less than filial love.
What joy was mine to see thee once again,
Thee and thy dwelling, and a crowd of things
About its narrow precincts all beloved,
And many of them seeming yet my own !
Why should I speak of what a thousand hearts
Have felt, and every man alive can guess ?
The rooms, the court, the garden were not left
Long unsaluted, nor the sunny seat
Round the stone table under the dark pine,
Friendly to studious or to festive hours ;
Nor that unruly child of mountain birth,
The famous brook, who, soon as he was boxed
Within our garden, found himself at once,
As if by trick insidious and unkind,
Stripped of his voice and left to dimple down
(Without an effort and without a will)
A channel paved by man's officious care.
I looked at him and smiled, and smiled again,
And in the press of twenty thousand thoughts,
" Ha," quoth I, " pretty prisoner, are you there ! "
Well might sarcastic Fancy then have whispered,
" An emblem here behold of thy own life ;
In its late course of even days with all
Their smooth enthralment ; " but the heart was full,
Too full for that reproach.   My aged Dame
Walked proudly at my side : she guided me ;
I willing, nay—nay, wishing to be led.
—The face of every neighbour whom I met
Was like a volume to me ; some were hailed
Upon the road, some busy at their work,

Unceremonious greetings interchanged
With half the length of a long field between.
Among my schoolfellows I scattered round
Like recognitions, but with some constraint
Attended, doubtless, with a little pride,
But with more shame, for my habiliments,
The transformation wrought by gay attire.
Not less delighted did I take my place
At our domestic table : and, dear Friend !
In this endeavour simply to relate
A Poet's history, may I leave untold
The thankfulness with which I laid me down
In my accustomed bed, more welcome now
Perhaps than if it had been more desired
Or been more often thought of with regret ;
That lowly bed whence I had heard the wind
Roar, and the rain beat hard ; where I so oft
Had lain awake on summer nights to watch
The moon in splendour couched among the leaves
Of a tall ash, that near our cottage stood ;
Had watched her with fixed eyes while to and fro
In the dark summit of the waving tree
She rocked with every impulse of the breeze.[1]

One old friend from whom he received a hearty welcome on that memorable return to his well-loved haunts calls for passing mention —the " rough terrier " who had been his faithful companion in many a ramble.

Among the masters at Hawkshead there was one, the Rev. William Taylor, who, though he died while Wordsworth was still at school, and so passed early out of his life, left a deep im-

[1] "The Prelude," iv 27-92.

pression upon him.[1] He is particularly interesting to us here because he was in part the original of the Matthew of the poems, whom we know as a typical representative of Wordsworth's ideal of simple manhood and as an exponent of his elemental philosophy.

> The sighs which Matthew heaved were sighs
> Of one tired out with fun and madness ;
> The tears which came to Matthew's eyes
> Were tears of light, the dew of gladness.
>
> Yet, sometimes, when the secret cup
> Of still and serious thought went round,
> It seemed as if he drank it up—
> He felt with spirit so profound.[2]

Such was Matthew's " happy soul." Such had been Taylor's. We must remember, however, that while many of Taylor's characteristics enter into his composition, Matthew is confessedly an idealization. " Like the Wanderer in 'The Excursion,' this schoolmaster was made up of several, both of his class and men of other occupations."[3]

A boy of Wordsworth's disposition is certain to get much of his most valuable education from independent contact with things outside the class-room walls ; and it was fortunate for him, therefore, that the routine at Hawkshead left him plenty of opportunity to go his own way. If his schooldays were " very happy

[1] For a touching reference to his illness and death see " Address to the Scholars of the Village School of ——."
[2] " Matthew."
[3] Wordsworth's note to " Matthew "

ones," it was, he afterwards said, " chiefly because I was left at liberty then, and in the vacations, to read whatever books I liked. For example, I read all Fielding's works, ' Don Quixote,' ' Gil Blas,' and any part of Swift that I liked—' Gulliver's Travels ' and the ' Tale of the [*sic*] Tub ' being both much to my taste." There is nothing to show that his poetic genius was at all precocious. His first verses were composed as a task set by his master, the subject being " The Summer Vacation," though he was moved to add a sequel on his own account on " Return to School." " There was nothing," he declares, " remarkable in either poem ; but I was called upon among other scholars to write verses upon the completion of the second centenary from the foundation of the school in 1585 by Archbishop Sandys. These verses were much admired—far more than they deserved, for they were but a tame imitation of Pope's versification, and a little in his style."

As an example of the kind of verse which Wordsworth was capable of producing when a boy I will quote a passage from " Lines written as a School Exercise at Hawkshead, Anno Ætatis 14 " :

> When Superstition left the golden light
> And fled indignant to the shades of night ;
> When pure Religion reared the peaceful breast
> And lulled the warring passions into rest,
> Drove far away the savage thoughts that roll
> In the dark mansions of the bigot's soul,

Enlivening Hope displayed her cheerful ray,
And beamed on Britain's sons a brighter day ;
So when on Ocean's face the storm subsides,
Hushed are the winds and silent are the tides ;
The God of day, in all the pomp of light,
Moves through the vault of heaven, and dissipates
　　the night.

And so on and so on. These lines are well enough in their way, and their smoothness and correctness are rather remarkable. But they are of course in the conventional manner of the time ; they are purely imitative ; they are such as any clever boy of fourteen might have written ; and they certainly give no promise of unusual poetic powers in years to come. After this, however, his genius must soon have begun to grow, for we recognize a very different quality in the following :

EXTRACT

FROM THE CONCLUSION OF A POEM, COMPOSED
IN ANTICIPATION OF LEAVING SCHOOL

Dear native regions, I foretell,
From what I feel at this farewell,
That, wheresoe'er my steps may tend,
And whensoe'er my course shall end,
If in that hour a single tie
Survive of local sympathy,
My soul will cast the backward view,
The longing look alone on you.
Thus, while the Sun sinks down to rest
Far in the regions of the west,
Though to the vale no parting beam
Be given, not one memorial gleam,

WORDSWORTH & HIS POETRY

A lingering light he fondly throws
On the dear hills where first he rose.

Here there is the accent of truth and sincerity,
and Wordsworth was right in praising the
beauty of the closing image. It is interesting
to note that these lines were afterwards recast
in blank verse in "The Prelude." Wordsworth first describes the spot and the circumstances in which they were written, and then
proceeds to paraphrase the thoughts which
flowed "in a pure stream of words fresh from
the heart."

A grove there is whose boughs
Stretch from the western marge of Thurstonmere,
With length of shade so thick, that whoso glides
Along the line of low-roofed water, moves
As in a cloister.   Once—while, in that shade
Loitering, I watched the golden beams of light
Flung from the setting sun, as they reposed
In silent beauty on the naked ridge
Of a high eastern hill—thus flowed my thoughts
In a pure stream of words fresh from the heart :
Dear native Regions, wheresoe'er shall close
My mortal course, there will I think on you ;
Dying, will cast on you a backward look ;
Even as this setting sun (albeit the Vale
Is nowhere touched by one memorial gleam)
Doth with the fond remains of his last power
Still linger, and a farewell lustre sheds,
On the dear mountain-tops where first he rose.[1]

The quotation just made leads us directly to
what is incomparably the most potent element

[1] "The Prelude," viii. 458-475.

in Wordsworth's early education—the awakening of his love of nature. At first this was
only a healthy boy's love of the open air and
the freedom of the fields. Boating on Esthwaite Water in summer, skating on the frozen
lake in winter beneath the sparkling stars, long
rambles at dawn, nutting and bird's-nesting :
nature to begin with meant these things for
him as for his companions, and meant little
else.

> A boy I loved the sun,
> Not as I since have loved him, as a pledge
> And surety of our earthly life, a light
> Which we behold and feel we are alive ;
> Nor for his bounty to so many worlds—
> But for this cause, that I had seen him lay
> His beauty on the morning hills, had seen
> The western mountain touch his setting orb,
> In many a thoughtless hour, when, from excess
> Of happiness, my blood appeared to flow
> For its own pleasure, and I breathed with joy.[1]

But before long this animal love of nature
began to change into a love which was mystical
and spiritual. The " creative soul " awoke
and the world became alive for him with strange
hints and symbols. A new glory and a new
meaning stole across the face of familiar things,
and whispers came to him from afar which
seemed " most audible, then, when the fleshly
ear . . . forgot her functions, and slept undisturbed." This great transformation in his
relations with nature—this heightening and

[1] " The Prelude," ii. 178–188.

deepening of his primitive feelings—was, of course, gradual. There was also, as we shall see presently, an intermediate stage in his development. Yet certain experiences stood out as landmarks in his mind. One such is commemorated in the lines entitled " Nutting," originally intended for " The Prelude," but omitted " as not being wanted there." " These verses," Wordsworth told Miss Fenwick, " arose out of the remembrance of feelings I had often had when a boy." The expedition described was in object an ordinary nutting expedition only, and the lad set out in his oldest clothes and with wallet and crook, intent, as on many a former occasion, upon the ripe wealth of the hazel coppices he already knew so well. But while he was exulting in the results of his " merciless ravage," a sudden shock of pain gave him pause. He realized that he had somehow inflicted injury upon the life that was all about him and felt the reproof of the " silent trees " and " the intruding sky." This new sense of the life in nature—of the " spirit in the woods "—never afterwards forsook him.

NUTTING

It seems a day
(I speak of one from many singled out)
One of those heavenly days that cannot die ;
When, in the eagerness of boyish hope,
I left our cottage-threshold, sallying forth
With a huge wallet o'er my shoulders slung,
A nutting-crook in hand ; and turned my steps

24

WORDSWORTH & HIS POETRY

Tow'rd some far-distant wood, a Figure quaint,
Tricked out in proud disguise of cast-off weeds
Which for that service had been husbanded,
By exhortation of my frugal Dame—
Motley accoutrement, of power to smile
At thorns, and brakes, and brambles,—and, in truth,
More raggèd than need was ! O'er pathless rocks,
Through beds of matted fern, and tangled thickets,
Forcing my way, I came to one dear nook
Unvisited, where not a broken bough
Drooped with its withered leaves, ungracious sign
Of devastation ; but the hazels rose
Tall and erect, with tempting clusters hung,
A virgin scene !—A little while I stood,
Breathing with such suppression of the heart
As joy delights in ; and, with wise restraint
Voluptuous, fearless of a rival, eyed
The banquet ;—or beneath the trees I sate
Among the flowers, and with the flowers I played ;
A temper known to those, who, after long
And weary expectation, have been blest
With sudden happiness beyond all hope.
Perhaps it was a bower beneath whose leaves
The violets of five seasons re-appear
And fade, unseen by any human eye ;
Where fairy water-breaks do murmur on
For ever ; and I saw the sparkling foam,
And—with my cheek on one of those green stones
That, fleeced with moss, under the shady trees,
Lay round me, scattered like a flock of sheep—
I heard the murmur and the murmuring sound,
In that sweet mood when pleasure loves to pay
Tribute to ease ; and, of its joy secure,
The heart luxuriates with indifferent things,
Wasting its kindliness on stocks and stones,

And on the vacant air.   Then up I rose,
And dragged to earth both branch and bough, with
    crash
And merciless ravage : and the shady nook
Of hazels, and the green and mossy bower,
Deformed and sullied, patiently gave up
Their quiet being : and, unless I now
Confound my present feelings with the past ;
Ere from the mutilated bower I turned
Exulting, rich beyond the wealth of kings,
I felt a sense of pain when I beheld
The silent trees, and saw the intruding sky—
Then, dearest Maiden, move along these shades
In gentleness of heart ; with gentle hand
Touch— for there is a spirit in the woods.

Another noteworthy experience is recorded in
" The Prelude." One summer evening he
pushed out alone for a row on the lake.   It was
a stolen pleasure, and perhaps he thought to
enjoy it all the more on that account.   Absolute
stillness hung over the waters ;   above him
" was nothing but the stars and the grey sky " ;
beyond, a peak towered up " black and huge."
A great awe fell upon him as he rowed :

            I struck and struck again,
And growing still in stature the grim shape
Towered up between me and the stars, and still,
For so it seemed, with purpose of its own
And measured motion like a living thing,
Strode after me.   With trembling oars I turned,
And through the silent water stole my way
Back to the covert of the willow tree ;
There in her mooring-place I left my bark,—
And through the meadows homeward went, in grave

And serious mood ; but after I had seen
That spectacle, for many days, my brain
Worked with a dim and undetermined sense
Of unknown modes of being ; o'er my thoughts
There hung a darkness, call it solitude
Or blank desertion.[1]

An indistinct feeling was left with him of
something vast and mysterious.

No familiar shapes
Remained, no pleasant images of trees,
Of sea or sky, no colours of green fields ;
But huge and mighty forms, that do not live
Like living men, moved slowly through the mind
By day, and were a trouble to my dreams.[2]

Then follows a fine passage of recapitulation :

Wisdom and Spirit of the universe !
Thou Soul that art the eternity of thought
That givest to forms and images a breath
And everlasting motion, not in vain
By day or star-light thus from my first dawn
Of childhood didst thou intertwine for me
The passions that build up our human soul ;
Not with the mean and vulgar works of man,
But with high objects, with enduring things—
With life and nature—purifying thus
The elements of feeling and of thought,
And sanctifying, by such discipline,
Both pain and fear, until we recognise
A grandeur in the beatings of the heart.
Nor was this fellowship vouchsafed to me
With stinted kindness.   In November days,

----

[1] " The Prelude," i. 380-395.   [2] *Ibid.* 395-400.

When vapours rolling down the valley made
A lonely scene more lonesome, among woods,
At noon and 'mid the calm of summer nights,
When, by the margin of the trembling lake,
Beneath the gloomy hills homeward I went
In solitude, such intercourse was mine ;
Mine was it in the fields both day and night,
And by the waters, all the summer long.[1]

Through such experiences as these the spiritual significance of the universe was gradually revealed to him. " The earth and the common face of Nature " began to speak to him " rememberable things."

'Twere long to tell
What spring and autumn, what the winter snows,
And what the summer shade, what day and night,
Evening and morning, sleep and waking, thought
From sources inexhaustible, poured forth
To feed the spirit of religious love
In which I walked with Nature.[2]

His spiritual faculties, now quickened into activity, found their chief satisfaction in intimate communion with the indwelling spirit of external things, but in such communion the spiritual faculties were themselves the intermediaries and interpreters.

An auxiliar light
Came from my mind, which on the setting sun
Bestowed new splendour ; the melodious birds,
The fluttering breezes, fountains that run on

---

[1] " The Prelude," i. 401-424.   [2] *Ibid.* ii. 353-359.

Murmuring so sweetly in themselves, obeyed
A like dominion, and the midnight storm
Grew darker in the presence of my eye :
Hence my obeisance, my devotion hence,
And hence my transport.[1]

But perhaps the most decisive event in his early spiritual history occurred during that first summer vacation from Cambridge, of which I have already spoken. Though it carries us a little beyond the point actually reached in our story we may most fittingly deal with it here. It was, as will be seen, in the nature of a great awakening to a sense of his destiny and calling. Despite the stir of higher impulses he had allowed himself to be lured away by " heady schemes " and " trivial pleasures." Then came " a particular hour " of uplift and illumination which, as he was fain to believe, exercised a lasting influence over his life. He had been indulging in what to a youth of his austere temper seemed like " giddy revelry " :

'Mid a throng
Of maids and youths, old men, and matrons staid,
A medley of all tempers, I had passed
The night in dancing, gaiety, and mirth,
With din of instruments and shuffling feet,
And glancing forms, and tapers glittering,
And unaimed prattle flying up and down ;
Spirits upon the stretch, and here and there
Slight shocks of young love-liking interspersed,
Whose transient pleasure mounted to the head,
And tingled through the veins.

[1] " The Prelude," ii. 368-376.

29

This continued till dawn, for :

> Ere we retired,
> The cock had crowed, and now the eastern sky
> Was kindling, not unseen, from humble copse
> And open field, through which the pathway wound,
> And homeward led my steps.

Then came the never-to-be-forgotten solitary walk in the dewy freshness of the dawn :

> Magnificent
> The morning rose, in memorable pomp,
> Glorious as e'er I had beheld—in front,
> The sea lay laughing at a distance ; near,
> The solid mountains shone, bright as the clouds,
> Grain-tinctured, drenched in empyrean light ;
> And in the meadows and the lower grounds
> Was all the sweetness of a common dawn—
> Dews, vapours, and the melody of birds,
> And labourers going forth to till the fields.
> Ah ! need I say, dear Friend ! that to the brim
> My heart was full ; I made no vows, but vows
> Were then made for me ; bond unknown to me
> Was given, that I should be, else sinning greatly,
> A dedicated Spirit.[1]

The striking contrast between the noisy scene just left behind and the glories of sunrise over mountains, sea, and meadows, might well have impressed even a less sensitive mind than his. But for him it was fraught with an unmistakable and irresistible appeal. This was one of the formative moments of his life :

[1] " The Prelude," iv. 323–337.

WORDSWORTH & HIS POETRY

On I walked
In thankful blessedness, which yet survives.

It is well that we should dwell upon the early growth of Wordsworth's " religious love " of nature for the simple reason that we are here in touch with the essential principles of all his after-life. To that love, as he himself again and again averred, he was primarily indebted for guidance in the time of darkness and peril, for strength in need, for consolation in sorrow, for the deepest happiness he had ever been privileged to enjoy. Let one passage in testimony be here reproduced ; another, even more memorable, will follow presently :

> If in my youth I have been pure in heart,
> If, mingling with the world, I am content
> With my own modest pleasures, and have lived
> With God and Nature communing, removed
> From little enmities and low desires—
> The gift is yours ; if in these times of fear,
> This melancholy waste of hopes o'erthrown,
> If, 'mid indifference and apathy,
> And wicked exultation when good men
> On every side fall off, we know not how,
> To selfishness, disguised in gentle names
> Of peace and quiet and domestic love,
> Yet mingled not unwillingly with sneers
> On visionary minds ; if, in this time
> Of dereliction and dismay, I yet
> Despair not of our nature, but retain
> A more than Roman confidence, a faith
> That fails not, in all sorrow my support,
> The blessing of my life—the gift is yours,

Ye winds and sounding cataracts ! 'tis yours,
Ye mountains ! thine, O Nature !   Thou hast fed
My lofty speculations ; and in thee,
For this uneasy heart of ours, I find
A never-failing principle of joy
And purest passion.[1]

III

ON their father's death William and his brothers had passed into the care of two uncles, Richard Wordsworth and Christopher Crackenthorpe.   The Wordsworth family had not been left as well off as might have been expected from John Wordsworth's position, for Sir James Lowther, who had some time before borrowed £5000 from him, now refused to repay, and a good deal of the attorney's remaining fortune was wasted in vain efforts to recover the money.   In these circumstances the two guardians behaved with commendable generosity ;   they provided the funds necessary to keep the boys at Hawkshead, and when the time came sent two of them, William and Christopher, to complete their education at the university.

It was on a dreary morning in October 1787 that Wordsworth entered Cambridge.   He was in high spirits and "full of hope."   But he soon found that the university was uncongenial to him.   Its moral and intellectual atmosphere was dull and uninspiring.   The life led by the

---

[1] "The Prelude," ii. 427–450.

undergraduates was unprofitable and often worse. The prescribed routine of study was by no means to his taste, and academic distinction "but little sought" by him and "little won." Thrown largely upon himself he found refuge in nature and in his own soul, and began to discover "what independent solaces" were his "to mitigate the injurious sway of place and circumstance." Often leaving behind him "the crowd, buildings, and groves," he would wander alone about the "level fields," missing the mountains to which he had been accustomed, yet still well pleased to peruse "the common countenance of earth and sky"; [1] while evening after evening it was his habit, even in the depth of winter, to linger in the "college groves" and "tributary walks," brooding on many things. In books, too, he found cheering companionship, though his "over-love of freedom" prevented him from substituting any "settled plan" of reading for that laid down in the curriculum.[2] He read the great old English poets :

Beside the pleasant Mill of Trompington
I laughed with Chaucer in the hawthorn shade ;
Heard him, while birds were warbling, tell his tales
Of amorous passion. And that gentle Bard,
Chosen by the Muses for their Page of State—
Sweet Spenser, moving through his clouded heaven
With the moon's beauty and the moon's soft pace,
I called him Brother, Englishman, and Friend !
Yea, our blind Poet, who in his later day,

[1] "The Prelude," iii. 90 ff.   [2] *Ibid.* vi. 25 ff.

Stood almost single ; uttering odious truth—
Darkness before, and danger's voice behind,
Soul awful—if the earth has ever lodged
An awful soul—I seemed to see him here
Familiarly, and in his scholar's dress
Bounding before me, yet a stripling youth—
A boy, no better, with his rosy cheeks
Angelical, keen eye, courageous look,
And conscious step of purity and pride.[1]

Cervantes and Shakespeare were also added to his list of friends. One entire book of " The Prelude " is devoted to books and their influence, and in it Wordsworth breathes a blessing on all those " inspired souls " whose works " lay their sure foundations in the heart of man," from the Hebrew poets and " Homer the great Thunderer " down to the nameless ballad-singers whose " wren-like warblings " are the delight of " cottagers and spinners at the wheel."

His first college vacation he spent, as we have seen, among his " native hills." The following summer—that of 1789—he visited his grand-parents at Penrith, and there met his sister Dorothy, whom he had not seen for nearly four years.[2] There, too, he found " another maid, who also shed a gladness o'er that season "— his cousin Mary Hutchinson, who years before had been with him at a Dame School in Penrith, but who now first stirred tender feelings which were later to blossom into love. These two holidays were full of happiness. But his spirit was too restless to be satisfied even with such unalloyed pleasures as they afforded. He began to crave for wider horizons and a more varied knowledge of life ; and so when the third summer once more brought him freedom, he resolved upon spending it in a walking tour on the Continent. Such an enterprise would not be in the least surprising now. In Wordsworth's youth it was an "unprecedented course," upon which he did not enter without considerable misgivings. But his mind was made up and his plan was duly carried out. "Lightly equipped," says the poetic record—which, being translated into prose, means that each carried a stout stick and had all the "needments" for the journey "tied up in a pocket-handkerchief "—he and his "youthful friend," Robert Jones—" he, too, a mountaineer "—set out "side by side, bound to the distant Alps."

It was a moment of great expectancy among the nations, for the Revolution had brought the promise of a new and glorious era in the unfolding life of man.

> Europe at that time was thrilled with joy,
> France standing on the top of golden hours,
> And human nature seeming born again.[1]

The route which the young travellers had marked out lay through Burgundy, down the Rhone, by way of Savoy to Geneva, Villeneuve, Martigny and Chamounix, across the Alps by the Simplon as far as the Italian lakes, and thence back by Lucerne, Zurich, Schaffhausen,

[1] "The Prelude," vi. 339 341.

35

the Rhine and Cologne, and so through Belgium to Calais. They chanced to land in Calais on the 13th July, the eve of the first anniversary of the fall of the Bastille, and of " that great federal day " when the king was to swear allegiance to the new constitution ; and evidences of the wonderful enthusiasm which the Revolution had inspired met them at once on every side, for

> there we saw,
> In a mean city, and among a few,
> How bright a face is worn when joy of one
> Is joy for tens of millions.[1]

Then, striking south, they took their way through hamlets and towns " gaudy with reliques of that festival " ; " songs, garlands, mirth, banners, and happy faces " made their road gay ; [2] and even in " sequestered villages " they

> found benevolence and blessedness
> Spread like a fragrance everywhere, when spring
> Hath left no corner of the land untouched.

More than once they were witnesses of open-air " dances of liberty," and a little later, while sailing up the Rhone, fell in with a number of delegates returning

> From the great spousals newly solemnised
> At their chief city, in the sight of Heaven.[3]

All this was very exhilarating. Yet Words-

---

[1] " The Prelude," vi. 346–349.
[2] Sonnet : " Jones ! as from Calais southward you and I."
[3] " The Prelude," vi. 389–390.

worth was affected by these and other similar experiences less than might perhaps have been expected. For reasons which he himself will explain presently, nature and the wonders of " the ever-living Universe " interested him far more than political excitement and the awakened hopes of man. " A glorious time, a happy time " indeed it was, when "triumphant looks " were "the common language of all eyes." But

> A stripling, scarcely of the household then
> Of social life, I looked upon these things
> As from a distance ; heard, and saw, and felt,
> Was touched, but with no intimate concern.[1]

He rather turned from these to the " new delights " which bountiful nature spread round his steps " like sunshine o'er green fields."

IV

WORDSWORTH took his degree in January 1791, and left the university with no settled plans for the future. His relatives wanted him to enter the Church, but this he felt would be a mistake. He shrank from the law, which was also proposed, and though he was conscious of leanings towards the army, a military career was for several reasons out of the question.

In this state of uncertainty he drifted to London, where he spent some months in idleness. He wandered about the streets ; saw all the " sights " ; frequented the theatre ; heard

[1] " The Prelude," vi. 776-779.

the " brawls of lawyers in their courts " ;
listened to many sermons, not always to edifica-
tion ; and in the House of Commons was much
impressed by the oratory of Burke. Yet save
that he was moved to astonishment and grief
by the squalor, extravagance, and wickedness
of the great metropolis, this brief residence in
London influenced him but little. The spirit of
nature still haunted him in the city streets,[1] and
even amid the most sordid surroundings " the
Soul of Beauty and enduring Life. vouchsafed
her inspiration." Here undoubtedly we have
the germ of one of his early poems, " The
Reverie of Poor Susan." " This arose," he
said, " out of my observations of the affecting
music of these birds "—the caged thrushes—
" hanging in this way in the London streets
during the freshness and stillness of the spring
morning," and it crystallizes what must have
been a frequent experience with him during his
perambulations—the transforming power of a
sudden flash of memory and the vision which it
brings with it.[2]

THE REVERIE OF POOR SUSAN

At the corner of Wood Street, when daylight appears,
Hangs a Thrush that sings loud, it has sung for three
    years :
Poor Susan has passed by the spot, and has heard
In the silence of morning the song of the Bird.

[1] " The Prelude," vii. 765–771.
[2] This poem was, however, probably written somewhat later, during the
short visit which Wordsworth and Dorothy paid to their brother Richard in
London, in 1797.

WORDSWORTH & HIS POETRY

'Tis a note of enchantment ; what ails her ? She sees
A mountain ascending, a vision of trees ;
Bright volumes of vapour through Lothbury glide,
And a river flows on through the vale of Cheapside.

Green pastures she views in the midst of the dale,
Down which she so often has tripped with her pail ;
And a single small cottage, a nest like a dove's,
The one only dwelling on earth that she loves.

She looks, and her heart is in heaven : but they fade,
The mist and the river, the hill and the shade :
The stream will not flow, and the hill will not rise,
And the colours have all passed away from her eyes !

Still quite at sea regarding his prospects,
Wordsworth now determined to return to
France, this time, however, not for a brief visit
but for a lengthy sojourn. His immediate
purpose was the thorough mastery of the
French language. But we may surmise that he
was in part influenced by growing interest in
the French cause.

His " readiest course " to Orleans, which he
had selected as his place of residence, lay
through Paris, and there he remained a few
days, seeking out " each spot of old or recent
fame "—" the latter chiefly," as he signifi-
cantly adds. He listened to debates in the
National Assembly and the Hall of the Jacobins,
and " saw the Revolutionary Power toss like a
ship at anchor, rocked by storms." He wandered through the arcades of the Palais Royal,
and " stared and listened " while " hawkers

39

and haranguers " and " hissing **Factionists**
with ardent eyes " made " hubbub wild " about
him. He made a pilgrimage to the ruins of the
Bastille

> and from the rubbish gathered up a stone,
> And pocketed the relic, in the guise
> Of an enthusiast.[1]

Yet there was, he confesses, something rather
factitious about his emotion, and when he went
on to Orleans he was still, in a land which
" swarmed with passions " and amid all the
violent concussions of the hour, curiously
apathetic. Whence this indifference ? It was
due, he replies, in part to his failure, through
want of proper knowledge and insight, to realize
the portentous significance of what was taking
place ; but in part also to the fact that to one
of his temper and early training the Revolution
at that stage of its development seemed after
all very much a matter of course. He understood little indeed about the " nice distinctions
then on every tongue, of natural rights and
civil " ; the " acts of nations and their passing
interests " failed to move him ; but the great
essential principles of liberty, equality, and the
brotherhood of man were in his very blood.

> For, born in a poor district, and which yet
> Retaineth more of ancient homeliness,
> Than any other nook of English ground,
> It was my fortune scarcely to have seen,
> Through the whole tenor of my school-day time,

" The Prelude," ix. 69-71

The face of one, who, whether boy or man,
Was vested with attention or respect
Through claims of wealth or blood ; nor was it least
Of many benefits, in later years
Derived from academic institutes
And rules, that they held something up to view
Of a Republic, where all stood thus far
Upon equal ground ; that we were brothers all
In honour, as in one community,
Scholars and gentlemen ; where, furthermore,
Distinction open lay to all that came,
And wealth and titles were in less esteem
Than talents, worth, and prosperous industry.
Add unto this, subservience from the first
To presences of God's mysterious power
Made manifest in Nature's sovereignty,
And fellowship with venerable books,
To sanction the proud workings of the soul,
And mountain liberty.   It could not be
But that one tutored thus should look with awe
Upon the faculties of man, receive
Gladly the highest promises, and hail,
As best, the government of equal rights
And individual worth.   And hence, O Friend
If at the first great outbreak I rejoiced
Less than might well befit my youth, the cause
In part lay here, that unto me the events
Seemed nothing out of nature's certain course,
A gift that was come rather late than soon.[1]

A change of spirit occurred during his sojourn
at Orleans and Blois, between which places he
passed nearly a year.   He now became intimate
with " a band of military officers " of strongly

[1] "The Prelude," ix. 215–248.

WORDSWORTH & HIS POETRY

anti-revolutionary sentiments, and in his many
discussions with them the " zeal, which yet had
slumbered, now in opposition burst forth like a
Polar summer."[1]

Among them too, as it happened, was one
" of other mould "—a patriot and a zealous
supporter of the popular cause. This was
Michel Beaupuy, a man whose noble soul was
filled with the high and generous enthusiasm of
humanity. Towards the poor and the down-
trodden in particular his heart went out in
warmest sympathy.

> Man he loved
> As man ; and, to the mean ana the obscure,
> And all the homely in their homely works,
> Transferred a courtesy which had no air
> Of condescension.[2]

With this fine product and representative of
the early revolutionary faith, whose name, he
thought, was fully worthy to stand beside " the
worthiest of antiquity," Wordsworth formed a
close friendship, and together they often can-
vassed the great problems of government and
society. These endless talks exerted a profound
influence upon his mind. His " hatred of
absolute rule, where will of one is law of all,"
daily gained stronger hold upon him, and this
hatred had for its concomitant an ever-growing
love of and pity for " the abject multitude."
One day, in the course of their walk, he and
Beaupuy happened to meet " a hunger-bitten

girl " listlessly knitting " with pallid hands "
and leading by a cord tied to her arm a heifer
which, as it followed, picked a scanty meal
from the hedges by the wayside. This concrete
example of the misery of the masses of the
people touched Beaupuy's tender heart. " 'Tis
against that," he exclaimed, " that we are
fighting." And Wordsworth shared his faith
in the fundamental humanitarianism of the
revolutionary cause.

> I with him believed
> That a benignant spirit was abroad
> Which might not be withstood, that poverty
> Abject as this would in a little time
> Be found no more, that we should see the earth
> Unthwarted in her wish to recompense
> The meek, the lowly, patient child of toil,
> All institutes for ever blotted out
> That legalised exclusion, empty pomp
> Abolished, sensual state and cruel power
> Whether by edict of the one or few ;
> And finally, as sum and crown of all,
> Should see the people having a strong hand
> In framing their own laws ; whence better days
> To all mankind.[1]

Doubts and ominous forebodings at times
disturbed his faith. On his former visit to the
Continent he had been troubled by the expulsion
of the monks of the Chartreuse.[2] Now, as he

---

[1] " The Prelude," ix. 518–532.
[2] *Ibid.* vi. 420–435. It appears, however, that Wordsworth was in error
in supposing that the monks had been expelled. The soldiers whose invasion
of their solitude aroused his ire, were only making a " domiciliary visit."
See Legouis' " La Jeunesse de Wordsworth."

wandered along the banks of the Loire, and recalled all the romantic associations of that beautiful region, the violence of his political partisanship was checked for the moment by a vivid sense of the sanctity and charm of the past.[1] But such misgivings were only occasional. Wordsworth was now a " patriot " ; his heart was " all given to the people " and his " love was theirs " ; and, looking back, he recalls, in a passage of great general as well as personal interest, the splendid visionary enthusiasm of that wonderful era of faith and happiness.

> O pleasant exercise of hope and joy !
> For mighty were the auxiliars which then stood
> Upon our side, us who were strong in love !
> Bliss was it in that dawn to be alive,
> But to be young was very Heaven !   O times,
> In which the meagre, stale, forbidding ways
> Of custom, law, and statute, took at once
> The attraction of a country in romance !
> When Reason seemed the most to assert her rights
> When most intent on making of herself
> A prime enchantress—to assist the work,
> Which then was going forward in her name !
> Not favoured spots alone, but the whole Earth,
> The beauty wore of promise—that which sets
> [As at some moments might not be unfelt
> Among the bowers of Paradise itself)
> The budding rose above the rose full blown.
> What temper at the prospect did not wake
> To happiness unthought of ?   The inert
> Were roused, and lively natures rapt away !
> They who had fed their childhood upon dreams,

[1] " The Prelude," ix. 431–501.

The play-fellows of fancy, who had made
All powers of swiftness, subtilty, and strength
Their ministers,—who in lordly wise had stirred
Among the grandest objects of the sense,
And dealt with whatsoever they found there
As if they had within some lurking right
To wield it ;—they, too, who of gentle mood
Had watched all gentle motions, and to these
Had fitted their own thoughts, schemers more mild,
And in the region of their peaceful selves ;—
Now was it that *both* found, the meek and lofty
Did both find, helpers to their hearts' desire,
And stuff at hand, plastic as they could wish,—
Were called upon to exercise their skill,
Not in Utopia,—subterranean fields,—
Or some secreted island, Heaven knows where !
But in the very world, which is the world
Of all of us,—the place where, in the end,
We find our happiness, or not at all ! [1]

Wordsworth returned to Paris—" the fierce metropolis "—in October 1792, a month only after the September massacres. He had now come to believe that the salvation of France depended upon the Girondins, and lamenting their want of a vigorous policy, was on the point, despite the personal dangers to be incurred, of throwing in his lot with them. By this time, however, his relatives at home were becoming seriously alarmed on his own account, and felt it necessary to interfere. In his poetic record he speaks vaguely of having been " dragged " away from France " by a chain of

---

[1] " The Prelude," xi. 105-145.

45

harsh necessity.'' The crude fact is that his sup-
plies were now cut off. It was well for Wordsworth and for us that he was thus compelled to
return to England, and he himself afterwards
acknowledged thankfully that what seemed
'' harsh necessity '' was really '' the gracious
providence of Heaven.'' Had he been allowed
his own way, he would almost certainly have
perished at the hands of the Jacobins in the
general destruction of the Brissotin party.

V

IN England he found conservative opinion
running strongly against the Revolution,
the defence of which he accordingly
undertook in a letter to the Bishop of Llandaff.
One argument which he was accustomed to use
at this time, to the effect that the abuses which
attended the popular upheaval should really be
regarded as an evil heritage of the past, he
afterwards restated in '' The Prelude '':

> When a taunt
> Was taken up by scoffers in their pride,
> Saying, '' Behold the harvest that we reap
> From popular government and equality,''
> I clearly saw that neither these nor aught
> Of wild belief engrafted on their names
> By false philosophy had caused the woe,
> But a terrific reservoir of guilt
> And ignorance filled up from age to age,
> That could no longer hold its loathsome charge,
> But burst and spread in deluge through the land.[1]

[1] '' The Prelude,'' x. 470–480

WORDSWORTH & HIS POETRY

For the moment he thus stood firm in his revolutionary faith. But before long he found himself involved in a fierce struggle of conflicting motives. Pitt's declaration of war against France was a terrible shock to him— the first great shock his moral nature had ever received. He loved his country, yet, convinced that his country was now in the wrong, he felt himself compelled to rejoice when disaster overtook the British arms. Then came the Reign of Terror, which overwhelmed him with despair, and the ghastly thought of which long afterwards continued to torture him by day and to haunt his dreams by night. His hopes revived a little when news came of the fall of Robespierre.[1] But it was only for a brief time. The further course of events in France quickly alienated his sympathies, and when the Republic, still professing to act upon the principles of liberty, equality, and fraternity, entered upon a policy of military aggression, his " genial feelings " were turned to bitterness. For a time, even though France had failed him, he clung desperately to the abstract political theories behind the revolutionary movement ; deeply influenced in this, like many of his contemporaries, by the teachings of that remarkable man, William Godwin, in his " Enquiry concerning Political Justice." But he found little comfort in abstractions amid the wreck of concrete hopes. Little by little he began to recognize that he was on the wrong path. There was

[1] " The Prelude," x. 553–575.

47

nothing for it but to start afresh. In a thoroughly Godwinian spirit he determined to "anatomize the frame of social life" and to bring "all precepts, judgments, maxims, creeds" to the bar of reason. As might have been anticipated, the result was only confusion worse confounded. Bewildered and perplexed he now fell into intellectual despair. He had lost his bearings and was completely adrift.

In this great spiritual crisis his salvation— " thanks to the bounteous Giver of all good "— was wrought largely through the influence of his sister. She revived for him " a saving intercourse " with his " true self." [1] Her companionship brought back to him faith and peace. In particular, she restored him to nature, whose beauty and benign power had been forgotten amid all the excitement and strain through which he had lately passed. Even when they were children together his indebtedness to her had been incalculable :

> She gave me eyes, she gave me ears ;
> And humble cares, and delicate fears ;
> A heart, the fountain of sweet tears ;
> And love, and thought, and joy.[2]

These gifts she now renewed, and it was mainly through her mediation that " Nature's self " led him back " through opening day " to that perfect trust in the divine ordering of the world which was hereafter to be his solace and stay amid all the vicissitudes of life.

[1] " The Prelude," xi. 333 ff. [2] " The Sparrow's Nest."

Yet though Dorothy's influence was undoubtedly the most powerful personal factor in Wordsworth's restoration to spiritual health, that of Mary Hutchinson must not be forgotten.

> She came, no more a phantom to adorn
> A moment, but an inmate of the heart,
> And yet a spirit, there for me enshrined
> To penetrate the lofty and the low ;
> Even as one essence of pervading light
> Shines, in the brightest of ten thousand stars
> And the meek worm that feeds her lonely lamp
> Couched in the dewy grass.[1]

These lines recall the exquisite little poem which Wordsworth wrote about Mary two years after their marriage :

> She was a Phantom of delight
> When first she gleamed upon my sight ;
> A lovely Apparition, sent
> To be a moment's ornament ;
> Her eyes as stars of Twilight fair ;
> Like Twilight's, too, her dusky hair ;
> But all things else about her drawn
> From May-time and the cheerful Dawn ;
> A dancing Shape, an Image gay,
> To haunt, to startle, and way-lay.
>
> I saw her upon nearer view,
> A Spirit, yet a Woman too !
> Her household motions light and free,
> And steps of virgin-liberty ;
> A countenance in which did meet
> Sweet records, promises as sweet ;

[1] "The Prelude," xiv. 268–275.

D

A Creature not too bright or good
For human nature's daily food ;
For transient sorrows, simple wiles,
Praise, blame, love, kisses, tears, and smiles.

And now I see with eye serene
The very pulse of the machine ;
A Being breathing thoughtful breath,
A Traveller between life and death ;
The reason firm, the temperate will,
Endurance, foresight, strength, and skill ;
A perfect Woman, nobly planned,
To warn, to comfort, and command ;
And yet a Spirit still, and bright
With something of angelic light.

VI

IN February 1794 Wordsworth wrote to a
friend : " I have been doing nothing,
and still continue to do nothing. What
is to become of me I know not." The statement
that he had been doing nothing is not strictly
correct. He had been doing something—he had
made a definite start as a poet with the publication the preceding year of two poems " An
Evening Walk " and " Descriptive Sketches."
The former deals with the landscape of the
familiar region round Hawkshead and Ambleside, though as Wordsworth was careful to
note, it was not " confined to a particular walk
or an individual place—a proof (of which I was
unconscious at the time) of my unwillingness
to submit the poetic spirit to the chains of fact

and mere circumstance.'' [1] The latter is composed of scenes from his '' pedestrian tour among the Alps with Robert Jones,'' to whom it is dedicated. Both poems are in the orthodox '' classic '' couplet ; and in both there is much to remind us of the current poetic style. Such a passage as this, for example, from '' An Evening Walk,'' is unmistakably reminiscent of Goldsmith :

Far from my dearest Friend, 'tis mine to rove
Through bare grey dell, high wood, and pastoral cove ;
Where Derwent rests, and listens to the roar
That stuns the tremulous cliffs of high Lodore ;
Where peace to Grasmere's lonely island leads,
To willowy hedge-rows, and to emerald meads ;
Leads to her bridge, rude church, and cottaged grounds,
Her rocky sheepwalks, and her woodland bounds ;
Where, undisturbed by winds, Winander sleeps
'Mid clustering isles, and holly-sprinkled steeps ;
Where twilight glens endear my Esthwaite's shore,
And memory of departed pleasures, more.

It is only when we read these poems more closely that we are able to detect beneath their conventional mannerisms a certain distinctive

---

[1] It should never be forgotten that, notwithstanding his minute attention to fact, Wordsworth was opposed to anything approaching photographic literalism in descriptive poetry. Aubrey de Vere records a conversation with him in which he emphatically condemned the ultra-realistic method of poets who went to nature with '' pencil and notebook, and jotted down whatever struck them most.'' Nature, he declared, '' does not permit an inventory to be made of her charms.'' The poet should leave pencil and note-book at home ; and, as he walks, should fix his eye with a reverent attention upon the things about him. Afterwards he would find that he had forgotten much ; but '' that which remained, the picture surviving in the mind, would have presented the ideal and essential truth of the scene. . . . In every scene many of the most brilliant details are but accidental.''

51

and personal quality, particularly in their handling of nature. Both contain a large amount of carefully accumulated detail, while the specific character of the descriptions brings them into sharp contrast with the common class of eighteenth-century landscape verse. This is a point upon which long afterwards Wordsworth himself laid great stress. The eighteenth-century poet had been satisfied as a rule with vague generalizations. He, on the contrary, had endeavoured to " look steadily " at his subject and to reproduce the essential features of what he had seen. Speaking of " An Evening Walk," he said : " There is not an image in it which I have not observed ; and now, in my seventy-third year, I recollect the time and place where most of them were noticed." It is such direct and intimate rendering of nature which gives prophetic interest to this otherwise rather imitative early work. Take, for instance, the two lines which he himself picked out as marking a stage in his poetic development :

> And, fronting the bright west, yon oak entwines
> Its darkening boughs and leaves, in stronger lines.

On casual perusal this couplet may not appear in the least remarkable. Wordsworth's comment brings out its significance. " This is feebly and imperfectly expressed, but I recollect distinctly the very spot where this first struck me. It was on the way between Hawkshead and Ambleside, and gave me extreme pleasure.

52

WORDSWORTH & HIS POETRY

The moment was important in my poetical history, for I date from it my consciousness of the infinite variety of natural appearances which had been unnoticed by the poets of any age or country, so far as I was acquainted with them, and I made a resolution to supply, in some degree, the deficiency.'' Pope, with Walsh's aid, early learned that it was his mission to be a '' correct '' poet. Wordsworth, prompted by his own native genius, resolved in youth that he would become an interpreter of nature.

These poems attracted no attention, though at Cambridge they were read by Coleridge, who perceived in them the sign of fresh and original power.[1] From the point of view of profit or advancement, therefore, they might just as well have been kept in manuscript. Otherwise his outlook remained absolutely blank. There was thus good reason for his disquietude. He thought for a time of seeking an opening in journalism, and even of starting on his own account a monthly magazine, of mildly republican colour, to be called '' The Philanthropist.'' This, however, was never anything more than a dream. Restless, full of vague longings, but without definite plan or purpose, he continued to lead '' an undomestic wanderer's life,'' partly in London, partly among '' rural England's cultivated vales and Cambrian solitudes.'' [2] Then suddenly the pressing problem of his future was solved for him. Early in 1795 a young friend, Raisley Calvert, died of

[1] '' The Prelude,'' xiii. 352–365.   [2] *Ibid.* xiii. 350–354.

consumption, leaving him a legacy of £900, together with a message that he did so believing that, relieved from immediate anxieties and free to devote himself to literature, Wordsworth might use his powers and attainments for the benefit of mankind. By this thoughtful act his friend " cleared a passage " for him, and allowed the stream of his life to flow " in the bent of nature." Wordsworth was of course deeply moved, and some years later he enshrined his gratitude in the following beautiful sonnet :

TO THE MEMORY OF RAISLEY CALVERT [1]

Calvert ! it must not be unheard by them
Who may respect my name, that I to thee
Owed many years of early liberty.
This care was thine when sickness did condemn
Thy youth to hopeless wasting, root and stem—
That I, if frugal and severe, might stray
Where'er I liked ; and finally array
My temples with the Muse's diadem.
Hence, if in freedom I have loved the truth ;
If there be aught of pure, or good, or great,
In my past verse ; or shall be, in the lays
Of higher mood, which now I meditate ;—
It gladdens me, O worthy, short-lived, Youth !
To think how much of this will be thy praise.

The legacy was not large, but to Wordsworth it spelt independence. He sent at once for Dorothy, and brother and sister, who thereafter were always to live together till the former's death, started joint housekeeping at Racedown

[1] Cp. " The Prelude," xiv. 348–369,

54

Lodge, Dorsetshire, among the hills between Crewkerne and Lyme Regis. The place was lent to them, rent-free, by a Mr. Pinney of Bristol, a friend of Basil Montagu, who had known Wordsworth at Cambridge. Montagu also sent his little son to Racedown as Wordsworth's pupil, and this made a welcome addition to their slender income. Altogether, as Dorothy wrote to a friend, they had now between £70 and £80 a year to live on.

They stayed at Racedown nearly two years, leading a life of primitive simplicity, reading, writing, gardening, and taking long walks together amid the beautiful Dorset scenery : " as happy," Dorothy declared, " as human beings can be." This was the period of Wordsworth's recovery from the reaction which had followed upon the collapse of his revolutionary hopes. Through many hours of quiet intercourse with his sister and of solitary communings with nature and his own soul, the confidence he had lost in life's divine purpose and meaning came back to him, and with it peace and joy. In the fourth book of " The Excursion "—" Despondency Corrected "—he speaks at length through the mouth of the Wanderer of the influences which had been most potent in this restoration, and emphasizes in particular the primary importance of that religious faith which he had now regained :

> " One adequate support
> For the calamities of mortal life
> Exists—one only ; an assured belief

55

That the procession of our fate, howe'er
Sad or disturbed, is ordered by a Being
Of infinite benevolence and power ;
Whose everlasting purposes embrace
All accidents, converting them to good.
—The darts of anguish *fix* not where the seat
Of suffering hath been thoroughly fortified
By acquiescence in the Will supreme
For time and for eternity ; by faith,
Faith absolute in God, including hope,
And the defence that lies in boundless love
Of his perfections ; with habitual dread
Of aught unworthily conceived, endured
Impatiently, ill-done, or left undone,
To the dishonour of his holy name.
Soul of our Souls, and safeguard of the world !
Sustain, thou only canst, the sick of heart ;
Restore their languid spirits, and recall
Their lost affections unto thee and thine ! "

During these two years, while he laid up
much material for future use, Wordsworth
produced but little. But he worked at a
tragedy entitled " The Borderers," which was
later very properly rejected by the managers of
Covent Garden as " not calculated for the stage,"
and wrote two narrative poems, " Guilt and
Sorrow" and "Margaret, or The Ruined
Cottage." The former, a gloomy tale told in
Spenserian stanzas, is chiefly interesting because,
like a great deal of other literature inspired by
the humanitarian spirit of the revolutionary
age, it treats of the wrongs suffered by the poor
at the hands of constituted society. The latter,
which was afterwards incorporated in the open-
56

ing book of " The Excursion," is the first piece
of work done by Wordsworth which gave any
clear indication of his characteristic powers.

The beginning of his friendship with Coleridge
dates from this time. That brilliant genius and
weak-willed dreamer had already commenced
his fatal course of drifting, and now drifted to
Racedown, the inmates of which he took by
storm. Dorothy instantly discovered that he
was " a wonderful man." At first indeed she
thought him plain, with his pale face, wide
mouth, flabby lips, indifferent teeth, and
" longish, loose-flowing, half-curling, rough
black hair." But the moment he began to
talk his expression changed, his grey eyes
lighted up with celestial fire, and all his physical
peculiarities were forgotten under the magic of
his eloquence. He and Wordsworth quickly
found that they were brothers in spirit, and at
once began to exchange confidences. " The
first thing that was read after he came,"
Dorothy tells us, " was William's new poem,
' Ruined Cottage,' with which he was much
delighted ; and after tea he repeated to us two
acts and a half of his tragedy, ' Osorio.' The
next morning William read his tragedy ' The
Borderers ' "—which, it is surprising to learn,
Coleridge compared favourably with the work
of Shakespeare.[1] Thus a new influence was
introduced into Wordsworth's life which, according to his own statement, was second only to
that of his sister.

[1] See his letter to Cottle, June 1797, in " Letters of Coleridge," 1221.

VII

IN July 1797 the Wordsworths paid a visit to Coleridge, who was then living at Nether Stowey in Somersetshire, and finding a furnished house vacant in the Quantock Hills, about three miles away, they took it at once for the pleasure of being near their friend. Alfoxden, as the house was called, was a large country mansion, with extensive gardens, stables, and furniture enough for a dozen families ; yet, lest it should be supposed that such an establishment was as much beyond their means as it was admittedly in excess of their requirements, let it here be put on record that they obtained it at the fabulous rental of £23 a year, free of rates and taxes ! There they remained till June 1798. The country round about was an unfailing source of delight to them : "there is everything here," Dorothy wrote, "sea, woods as wild as fancy ever painted, brooks clear and pebbly as in Cumberland, villages so romantic." Amid such surroundings they could not fail to be happy. Two short poems belonging to the early months of 1798 are redolent of the charm of the neighbourhood and of Wordsworth's own quiet joy in all its details. The first, "composed in front of Alfoxden House " and addressed to Dorothy, is a call to the open : the "Edward" of the verses, by whom they were sent, being the little son of Basil Montagu.

TO MY SISTER

It is the first mild day of March :
Each minute sweeter than before,
The redbreast sings from the tall larch
That stands beside our door.

There is a blessing in the air,
Which seems a sense of joy to yield
To the bare trees, and mountains bare,
And grass in the green field.

My sister ! ('tis a wish of mine)
Now that our morning meal is done,
Make haste, your morning task resign ;
Come forth and feel the sun.

Edward will come with you ;—and, pray,
Put on with speed your woodland dress ;
And bring no book : for this one day
We'll give to idleness.

No joyless forms shall regulate
Our living calendar :
We from to-day, my Friend, will date
The opening of the year.

Love, now a universal birth,
From heart to heart is stealing,
From earth to man, from man to earth :
—It is the hour of feeling.

One moment now may give us more
Than years of toiling reason :
Our minds shall drink at every pore
The spirit of the season.

Some silent laws our hearts will make,
Which they shall long obey :
We for the year to come may take
Our temper from to-day.

And from the blessed power that rolls
About, below, above,
We'll frame the measure of our souls :
They shall be tuned to love.

Then come, my Sister ! come, I pray,
With speed put on your woodland dress ;
And bring no book : for this one day
We'll give to idleness.

The second poem is not marked by the same
abandonment of mind. The poet, brooding in
solitude, is touched by the thought of the
sufferings of humanity, and the note of sadness
steals in as he contrasts " Nature's holy plan "
with " what man has made of man." It was
" actually composed " while he " was sitting
by the side of the brook that runs . . . through
the grounds of Alfoxden." This Alfoxden dell,
he says, was one of his chosen resorts. It was
a chosen resort also of Coleridge, who describes
it in his poem, " This Lime Tree Bower my
Prison," written while Charles Lamb was on a
visit to Nether Stowey.

LINES WRITTEN IN EARLY SPRING

I heard a thousand blended notes,
While in a grove I sate reclined,
In that sweet mood when pleasant thoughts
Bring sad thoughts to the mind.

To her fair works did Nature link
The human soul that through me ran ;
And much it grieved my heart to think
What man has made of man.

Through primrose tufts, in that green bower,
The periwinkle trailed its wreaths ;
And 'tis my faith that every flower
Enjoys the air it breathes.

The birds around me hopped and played,
Their thoughts I cannot measure :—
But the least motion which they made
It seemed a thrill of pleasure.

The budding twigs spread out their fan,
To catch the breezy air ;
And I must think, do all I can,
That there was pleasure there.

If this belief from heaven be sent,
If such be Nature's holy plan,
Have I not reason to lament
What man has made of man ?

Coleridge's society, which, as Dorothy said,
had been the " principal inducement " to the
settlement at Alfoxden, proved a great stimulus
to Wordsworth's genius during the eleven
memorable months of their residence there.
" We are," Coleridge declared, " three people
with only one soul "—it is a pity that the
spiritual brotherhood was not a quartette instead
of a trio ; but poor Mrs. Coleridge did not seem
to count. In their long walks together over

hill and through wood, and in their many happy days of companionship, now at Alfoxden and now at Stowey, the talk of the two young men ran incessantly upon poetry, and many big plans of work were discussed which were destined to come to nothing : Coleridge, then as always, being specially fertile in schemes which were never to be carried out. One enterprise, however, arose out of their intercourse which, though apparently not in the least big, was fraught with immense consequences for literature. This was the production of the slender volume entitled " Lyrical Ballads," the publication of which is rightly regarded as opening a new chapter in the history of English poetry.

The origin of " Lyrical Ballads " is described by Coleridge in a passage which, well known as it is, must here be quoted once again.

During the first year that Mr. Wordsworth and I were neighbours, our conversations turned frequently on the two cardinal points of poetry, the power of exciting the sympathy of the reader by a faithful adherence to the truth of nature and the power of giving the interest of novelty by the modifying colours of imagination. . . . The thought suggested itself (to which of us I do not recollect) that a series of poems might be composed of two sorts. In the one, the incidents and agents were to be, in part at least, supernatural ; and the excellence aimed at was to consist in the interesting of the affections by the dramatic truth of such emotions as would naturally accompany such situations, supposing them real. . . . For the

62

second class, subjects were to be chosen from ordinary life ; the characters and incidents were to be such as will be found in every village and its vicinity where there is a meditative and feeling mind to seek after them, or to notice them when they present themselves.

In this idea originated the plan of the " Lyrical Ballads," in which it was agreed that my endeavours should be directed to persons and characters supernatural, or at least romantic, yet so as to transfer from our inward nature a human interest and a semblance of truth sufficient to procure for these shadows of imagination that willing suspension of disbelief for the moment which constitutes poetic faith. Mr. Wordsworth, on the other hand, was to propose to himself as his object, to give the charm of novelty to things of every day, and to excite a feeling analogous to the supernatural, by awakening the mind's attention to the lethargy of custom and directing it to the loveliness and wonders of the world before us : an inexhaustible treasure, but for which, in consequence of the film of familiarity and selfish solicitude, we have eyes, yet see not, ears that hear not, and hearts that neither feel nor understand.[1]

This passage enables us to appreciate the epoch-making character of the little book. It marks the culmination and the confluence of two tendencies which had been growing side by side during the later eighteenth century : the tendency towards romance, on the one hand, and, on the other, that towards naturalism, or simplicity in theme and treatment. With Coleridge's own contribution to the joint under-

[1] " Biographia Literaria, chap. xiv.

taking we have now nothing to do. Our concern is with Wordsworth's share, and particularly, for the moment, with such poems as "The Idiot Boy," "We are Seven," "The Thorn," and "Goody Blake and Harry Gill," which were designed as experiments in the poetical rendering of subjects hitherto deemed beneath the dignity of the muse.

٠ "The principal object, then, proposed in these poems," Wordsworth wrote two years later, "was to choose incidents and situations from common life, and to relate or describe them throughout, as far as was possible, in a selection of language actually used by men, and, at the same time, to throw over them a certain colouring of imagination, whereby ordinary things should be presented to the mind in an unusual aspect "; and he goes on to explain that "humble and rustic life was generally chosen, because in that condition the essential passions of the heart find a better soil in which they can attain their maturity, and are less under restraint, and speak a plainer and more emphatic language; because in that condition of life our elementary feelings co-exist in a state of greater simplicity, and, consequently, may be more accurately contemplated and more forcibly communicated; because the manners of rural life germinate from these elementary feelings, and, from the necessary character of rural occupations, are more easily comprehended, and are more durable; and, lastly, because in that condition the passions of men are incorporated with the beautiful and permanent forms of nature." [1]

In this remarkable declaration of faith there are many matters worthy of attention. I will here touch upon two only.

The first is the emphasis thrown upon the elementary character of the subjects dealt with. Whether Wordsworth was right or wrong in contending that essential humanity flourishes more fully in the country than in the city, and among the humble classes than in circles of greater refinement and culture, we need not now consider. The point to seize is, his desire to penetrate through the artificial trappings and transitory interests of civilization to that which is common to men as men and belongs to the permanent foundations of human life.

Then, secondly, there is his determination to bring the language of poetry back to naturalness and simplicity. Here he is in open revolt against the fashionable practice of the followers of the Augustan school, with their conventional mannerisms, their pompous circumlocutions, " their gaudiness and inane phraseology." In his attack upon the stereotyped formalism and empty rhetoric by which English poetry had long been vitiated Wordsworth obviously carried reaction a great deal too far. Poetry, according to his theory, should be written, as far as possible (it is unfortunate that he did not attempt to measure the saving grace of this

[1] Preface to second edition of " Lyrical Ballads," 1800. Cp. " The Excursion," i. 343–347.

qualification), in the simplest language of ordinary rustic folk—or, to be exact, in a selection of such language. It was, we must suppose, in the pursuit of this theory, unchecked by any sense of humour, that he was led to perpetrate those deplorable puerilities which gave the unregenerate occasion to scoff ; as when he wrote of " Simon Lee " :

> For still, the more he works, the more
> Do his weak ankles swell ;

and of Poor Betty :

> This piteous news so much it shocked her,
> She quite forgot to send the doctor
> To comfort poor old Susan Gale.

Theory, too, must be held responsible for the dreadful ineptitude of " We are Seven," for the " Idiot Boy," for " The Thorn," for " Goody Blake and Harry Gill " :

> Oh ! what's the matter ? what's the matter ?
> What is't that ails young Harry Gill ?
> That evermore his teeth they chatter,
> Chatter, chatter, chatter still !
> Of waistcoats Harry has no lack,
> Good duffle grey, and flannel fine ;
> He has a blanket on his back,
> And coats enough to smother nine.
>
> In March, December, and in July,
> 'Tis all the same with Harry Gill ;
> The neighbours tell, and tell you truly,
> His teeth they chatter, chatter still.

At night, at morning, and at noon,
'Tis all the same with Harry Gill ;
Beneath the sun, beneath the moon,
His teeth they chatter, chatter still !

Young Harry was a lusty drover,
And who so stout of limb as he ?
His cheeks were red as ruddy clover ;
His voice was like the voice of three.
Old Goody Blake was old and poor ;
Ill fed she was, and thinly clad ;
And any man who passed her door
Might see how poor a hut she had.

All day she spun in her poor dwelling :
And then her three hours' work at night,
Alas ! 'twas hardly worth the telling,
It would not pay for candle-light.
Remote from sheltered village-green,
On a hill's northern side she dwelt,
Where from sea-blasts the hawthorns lean,
And hoary dews are slow to melt.

By the same fire to boil their pottage,
Two poor old Dames, as I have known,
Will often live in one small cottage ;
But she, poor Woman ! housed alone.
'Twas well enough when summer came,
The long, warm, lightsome summer-day,
Then at her door the *canty* Dame
Would sit, as any linnet, gay.

But when the ice our streams did fetter,
Oh then how her old bones would shake !
You would have said, if you had met her,
'Twas a hard time for Goody Blake.

Her evenings then were dull and dead :
Sad case it was, as you may think,
For very cold to go to bed ;
And then for cold not sleep a wink.

O joy for her ! whene'er in winter
The winds at night had made a rout ;
And scattered many a lusty splinter
And many a rotten bough about.
Yet never had she, well or sick,
As every man who knew her says,
A pile beforehand, turf or stick,
Enough to warm her for three days.

Such flat and trivial writing as this may of
course be held to represent the abuse of Wordsworth's doctrine. But as Coleridge conclusively
showed in his masterly inquiry into the whole
subject, that doctrine itself is radically unsound ;
since the language of poetry can never be
identical with that of actual life in Wordsworth's narrow acceptation of the phrase, nor,
certainly, is the best language for poetic purposes to be found on the lips of unlettered
rustics.[1] Hence it is fortunate that, save in a
few poems which were written expressly to
illustrate but which in fact disproved them,
formulated theories had little influence upon his
own production. It is not by reference to his
doctrine, as Mr. Myers has said, that the merits
of his poetry are to be explained. Indeed we
may go farther than this. Wordsworth often

---

[1] "Biographia Literaria," chap. xvii. Coleridge was quite right in
protesting against Wordsworth's critical phraseology as "equivocal."

wrote superbly ; and he often wrote in a stiff, heavy, pedestrian style. But neither in the one case nor in the other had doctrine anything to do with the quality of his work.

That doctrine is none the less of great importance on both historic and personal grounds. Apart from the fact that it helped to break down a vicious tradition and to reassert the claims of simplicity and truth, it is particularly noteworthy because, like the closely connected theory of the proper subject-matter of poetry, it brings into prominence the essentially democratic character of Wordsworth's genius and aims. He had by this time rejected root and branch his early revolutionary creed, and reaction against that creed was presently to carry him, as we shall see in due course, to extreme conservatism. Yet his work still remains a part of the great revolutionary movement of the age. That movement was inspired by men's growing impatience of artifice, convention, and shams, by a desire to get " back to nature "—to fact and reality—and by an ever-widening sense of the value of that fundamental manhood which underlies all class distinctions and is one and the same in lettered and unlettered, in peer and ploughman. When Wordsworth declared that his chosen theme was to be " no other than the very heart of man " and " men as they are men within themselves," [1] when he sought his types of strong and noble character in the Cumberland shepherd, the

[1] " The Prelude," xiii. 231 ff.

pedlar, the leech-gatherer, he stood out as the poetic interpreter of the new democratic faith. When he conceived it as his chief mission, following the lead of nature herself, to conse-crate common things and " breathe grandeur upon the very humblest face of human life," [1] it was of this democratic faith that he was the mouthpiece and apostle. The tender feeling which overflowed from man to the lower animals, and moved him to think of the slain hart as part of the great brotherhood of God's creatures, was another aspect of the same faith.

> Grey-headed Shepherd, thou hast spoken well ;
> Small difference lies between thy creed and mine :
> This Beast not unobserved by Nature fell ;
> His death was mourned by sympathy divine.
>
> The Being, that is in the clouds and air,
> That is in the green leaves among the groves,
> Maintains a deep and reverential care
> For the unoffending creatures whom he loves.
>
> The pleasure-house is dust :—behind, before,
> This is no common waste, no common gloom ;
> But Nature, in due course of time, once more
> Shall here put on her beauty and her bloom.
>
> She leaves these objects to a slow decay,
> That what we are, and have been, may be known ;
> But at the coming of the milder day,
> These monuments shall all be overgrown.

[1] " The Prelude," xiii. 279 ff.

WORDSWORTH & HIS POETRY

> One lesson, Shepherd, let us two divide,
> Taught both by what she shows, and what conceals ;
> Never to blend our pleasure or our pride
> With sorrow of the meanest thing that feels.[1]

So again with his extravagant theories of poetic style. The language of poetry had long been the language of a caste. In his heroic attempt to break down the barriers of so-called art and to make poetry speak once more with the tongue of common men, the democratic inspiration is once more apparent.

VIII

ON June 26, 1798, the Wordsworths left Alfoxden, and after a short stay in Bristol, where their friend Joseph Cottle, the publisher, was busy with the " Lyrical Ballads,'' they set out on a walking tour along the banks of the Wye. That tour is memorable because it produced one of the greatest of Wordsworth's poems, the

LINES

COMPOSED A FEW MILES ABOVE TINTERN ABBEY, ON REVISITING THE BANKS OF THE WYE DURING A TOUR. JULY 13, 1798

Five years have past ; five summers, with the length
Of five long winters ! and again I hear
These waters, rolling from their mountain-springs
With a soft inland murmur.—Once again
Do I behold these steep and lofty cliffs,

[1] " Hart-Leap Well."

That on a wild secluded scene impress
Thoughts of more deep seclusion ; and connect
The landscape with the quiet of the sky.
The day is come when I again repose
Here, under this dark sycamore, and view
These plots of cottage-ground, these orchard-tufts,
Which at this season, with their unripe fruits,
Are clad in one green hue, and lose themselves
'Mid groves and copses.   Once again I see
These hedge-rows, hardly hedge-rows, little lines
Of sportive wood run wild : these pastoral farms,
Green to the very door ; and wreaths of smoke
Sent up, in silence, from among the trees !
With some uncertain notice, as might seem
Of vagrant dwellers in the houseless woods,
Or of some Hermit's cave, where by his fire
The Hermit sits alone.
                      These beauteous forms,
Through a long absence, have not been to me
As is a landscape to a blind man's eye :
But oft, in lonely rooms, and 'mid the din
Of towns and cities, I have owed to them
In hours of weariness, sensations sweet,
Felt in the blood, and felt along the heart ;
And passing even into my purer mind,
With tranquil restoration :   feelings too
Of unremembered pleasure : such, perhaps,
As have no slight or trivial influence
On that best portion of a good man's life,
His little, nameless, unremembered, acts
Of kindness and of love.   Nor less, I trust,
To them I may have owed another gift,
Of aspect more sublime ; that blessed mood,
In which the burthen of the mystery,
In which the heavy and the weary weight

WORDSWORTH & HIS POETRY

Of all this unintelligible world,
Is lightened :—that serene and blessed mood,
In which the affections gently lead us on,—
Until, the breath of this corporeal frame
And even the motion of our human blood
Almost suspended, we are laid asleep
In body, and become a living soul :
While with an eye made quiet by the power
Of harmony, and the deep power of joy,
We see into the life of things.
                                        If this
Be but a vain belief, yet, oh ! how oft—
In darkness and amid the many shapes
Of joyless daylight ; when the fretful stir
Unprofitable, and the fever of the world,
Have hung upon the beatings of my heart—
How oft, in spirit, have I turned to thee,
O sylvan Wye ! thou wanderer thro' the woods,
How often has my spirit turned to thee !
   And now, with gleams of half-extinguished thought,
With many recognitions dim and faint,
And somewhat of a sad perplexity,
The picture of the mind revives again :
While here I stand, not only with the sense
Of present pleasure, but with pleasing thoughts
That in this moment there is life and food
For future years.   And so I dare to hope,
Though changed, no doubt, from what I was when
      first
I came among these hills ; when like a roe
I bounded o'er the mountains, by the sides
Of the deep rivers, and the lonely streams,
Wherever nature led : more like a man
Flying from something that he dreads, than one
Who sought the thing he loved.   For nature then

(The coarser pleasures of my boyish days,
And their glad animal movements all gone by)
To me was all in all.—I cannot paint
What then I was.   The sounding cataract
Haunted me like a passion : the tall rock,
The mountain, and the deep and gloomy wood,
Their colours and their forms, were then to me
An appetite ; a feeling and a love,
That had no need of a remoter charm,
By thought supplied, nor any interest
Unborrowed from the eye.—That time is past,
And all its aching joys are now no more,
And all its dizzy raptures.   Not for this
Faint I, nor mourn nor murmur ; other gifts
Have followed ; for such loss, I would believe,
Abundant recompence.   For I have learned
To look on nature, not as in the hour
Of thoughtless youth ; but hearing oftentimes
The still, sad music of humanity,
Nor harsh nor grating, though of ample power
To chasten and subdue.   And I have felt
A presence that disturbs me with the joy
Of elevated thoughts ; a sense sublime
Of something far more deeply interfused,
Whose dwelling is the light of setting suns,
And the round ocean and the living air,
And the blue sky, and in the mind of man ;
A motion and a spirit, that impels
All thinking things, all objects of all thought,
And rolls through all things.   Therefore am I still
A lover of the meadows and the woods,
And mountains ; and of all that we behold
From this green earth ; of all the mighty world
Of eye, and ear, both what they half create,
And what perceive ; well pleased to recognise

WORDSWORTH & HIS POETRY

In nature and the language of the sense,
The anchor of my purest thoughts, the nurse,
The guide, the guardian of my heart, and soul
Of all my moral being.
                Nor perchance,
If I were not thus taught, should I the more
Suffer my genial spirits to decay :
For thou art with me here upon the banks
Of this fair river ; thou my dearest Friend,
My dear, dear Friend ; and in thy voice I catch
The language of my former heart, and read
My former pleasures in the shooting lights
Of thy wild eyes. Oh ! yet a little while
May I behold in thee what I was once,
My dear, dear Sister ! and this prayer I make,
Knowing that Nature never did betray
The heart that loved her ; 'tis her privilege,
Through all the years of this our life, to lead
From joy to joy : for she can so inform
The mind that is within us, so impress
With quietness and beauty, and so feed
With lofty thoughts, that neither evil tongues,
Rash judgments, nor the sneers of selfish men,
Nor greetings where no kindness is, nor all
The dreary intercourse of daily life,
Shall e'er prevail against us, or disturb
Our cheerful faith, that all which we behold
Is full of blessings. Therefore let the moon
Shine on thee in thy solitary walk ;
And let the misty mountain-winds be free
To blow against thee : and, in after years,
When these wild ecstasies shall be matured
Into a sober pleasure ; when thy mind
Shall be a mansion for all lovely forms,
Thy memory be as a dwelling-place

For all sweet sounds and harmonies ; oh ! then,
If solitude, or fear, or pain, or grief,
Should be thy portion, with what healing thoughts
Of tender joy wilt thou remember me,
And these my exhortations ! Nor, perchance—
If I should be where I no more can hear
Thy voice, nor catch from thy wild eyes these gleams
Of past existence—wilt thou then forget
That on the banks of this delightful stream
We stood together ; and that I, so long
A worshipper of Nature, hither came
Unwearied in that service : rather say
With warmer love—oh ! with far deeper zeal
Of holier love. Nor wilt thou then forget,
That after many wanderings, many years
Of absence, these steep woods and lofty cliffs,
And this green pastoral landscape, were to me
More dear, both for themselves and for thy sake !

With this wonderful poem before us we may
conveniently pause in our story to return to a
subject already opened up—Wordsworth's interpretation of nature.

It is important first of all to recall and still
further to specify the change which came over
his relations with nature as his knowledge of
life deepened and the " mellower years "
brought him " the philosophic mind." Three
stages in the growth of his love of nature are,
as will be observed, marked out in the foregoing
lines, which indeed state briefly what is set forth
at much greater length in " The Prelude."
First came, as we have already seen, the stage
in which the love of nature was, as I put it,
76

simply a healthy boy's delight in freedom and the open air. Then followed that intermediate period in which the sensuous beauty of nature was loved with an unreflecting passion altogether untouched by intellectual interests or associations—the kind of passion which found such full expression in the poetry of Keats.[1] Yet even this stage proved to be one of transition only. He passed beyond it, finding " abundant recompense " for whatever he may have lost by the way, into a mood of mind in which his love became profoundly religious in character. Here it is that we reach the distinctive quality in Wordsworth's nature poetry. Ardent devotion to natural beauty ; keenness of observation ; unfailing accuracy in the rendering of even the minutest details : these of course are important elements in his work. But they are not the most important. The essentially Wordsworthian feature of his treatment of nature is his intense spirituality.

We must not, however, suppose that though the " aching joys " and " dizzy raptures " of former years were now " no more," this intense spirituality was destructive of his simple delight in nature as nature. Aubrey de Vere has said that Wordsworth looked at nature as the mystic of old perused the page of Holy Writ, making little of the letter, but passing through it to the spiritual interpretation.[2] The state-

[1] Cp. my " Keats and his Poetry," in this series, pp. 35, 36.
[2] " On the Personal Character of Wordsworth's Poetry," in " Wordsworthiana," p. 147.

WORDSWORTH & HIS POETRY

ment is rather misleading. It cannot surely be maintained that Wordsworth made little of the letter. If the primrose by the river's brim was for him the symbol and index of divine things, it did not therefore cease to be the primrose. The spiritual meaning was added to the natural beauty, not substituted for it. As an expression of pure delight in such natural beauty the following verses could not easily be surpassed by any poet :

" I WANDERED LONELY AS A CLOUD "

I wandered lonely as a cloud
That floats on high o'er vales and hills,
When all at once I saw a crowd,
A host, of golden daffodils ;
Beside the lake, beneath the trees,
Fluttering and dancing in the breeze.

Continuous as the stars that shine
And twinkle on the milky way,
They stretched in never-ending line
Along the margin of a bay :
Ten thousand saw I at a glance,
Tossing their heads in sprightly dance.

The waves beside them danced ; but they
Out-did the sparkling waves in glee :
A poet could not but be gay,
In such a jocund company :
I gazed—and gazed—but little thought
What wealth the show to me had brought :

78

WORDSWORTH & HIS POETRY

For oft, when on my couch I lie
In vacant or in pensive mood,
They flash upon that inward eye⎤ [1]
Which is the bliss of solitude ; ⎦
And then my heart with pleasure fills,
And dances with the daffodils.

At the same time Aubrey de Vere is right in speaking of Wordsworth as a mystic, and his mysticism is such a fundamental and pervading element in his thought that it must be considered very carefully. Thoroughly anti-scientific and anti-rationalistic in temper, he was in radical opposition to all forms of philosophy which assume that the intellect is the only organ of truth. This is brought out clearly, for instance, in

A POET'S EPITAPH

Art thou a Statist in the van
Of public conflicts trained and bred ?
—First learn to love one living man ;
Then may'st thou think upon the dead.

A Lawyer art thou ?—draw not nigh !
Go, carry to some fitter place
The keenness of that practised eye,
The hardness of that sallow face.

Art thou a Man of purple cheer ?
A rosy Man, right plump to see ?
Approach ; yet, Doctor, not too near,
This grave no cushion is for thee.

[1] According to Wordsworth's own statement these two lines were contributed by his wife.

Or art thou one of gallant pride,
A Soldier and no man of chaff ?
Welcome !—but lay thy sword aside,
And lean upon a peasant's staff.

Physician art thou ? one, all eyes,
Philosopher ! a fingering slave,
One that would peep and botanise
Upon his mother's grave ?

Wrapt closely in thy sensual fleece,
O turn aside,—and take, I pray,
That he below may rest in peace,
Thy ever-dwindling soul, away !

A Moralist perchance appears ;
Led, Heaven knows how ! to this poor sod :
And he has neither eyes nor ears ;
Himself his world, and his own God ;

One to whose smooth-rubbed soul can cling
Nor form, nor feeling, great or small ;
A reasoning, self-sufficing thing,
An intellectual All-in-all !

Shut close the door ; press down the latch ;
Sleep in thy intellectual crust ;
Nor lose ten tickings of thy watch
Near this unprofitable dust.

But who is He, with modest looks,
And clad in homely russet brown ?
He murmurs near the running brooks
A music sweeter than their own.

WORDSWORTH & HIS POETRY

He is retired as noontide dew,
Or fountain in a noon-day grove ;
And you must love him, ere to you
He will seem worthy of your love.

The outward shows of sky and earth,
Of hill and valley, he has viewed ;
And impulses of deeper birth
Have come to him in solitude.

In common things that round us lie
Some random truths he can impart,—
The harvest of a quiet eye
That broods and sleeps on his own heart.

But he is weak ; both Man and Boy,
Hath been an idler in the land ;
Contented if he might enjoy
The things which others understand.

—Come hither in thy hour of strength ;
Come, weak as is a breaking wave !
Here stretch thy body at full length ;
Or build thy house upon this grave.

Thus there was for Wordsworth a world of
divine reality behind and within the ordinary
world of observation and experience—a world
to which mere reason would never give access,
but which was nevertheless open to the spiritual
faculty in man. Hints from this world come
to us from beyond the regions of time and
sense.

YES, IT WAS THE MOUNTAIN ECHO

Yes, it was the mountain Echo,
Solitary, clear, profound,
Answering to the shouting Cuckoo,
Giving to her sound for sound !

Unsolicited reply
To a babbling wanderer sent ;
Like her ordinary cry,
Like—but oh, how different !

Hears not also mortal Life ?
Hear not we, unthinking Creatures !
Slaves of folly, love, or strife—
Voices of two different natures ?

Have not *we* too ?—yes, we have
Answers, and we know not whence ;
Echoes from beyond the grave,
Recognised intelligence !

Such rebounds our inward ear
Catches sometimes from afar—
Listen, ponder, hold them dear ;
For of God,—of God they are.

With these simple, yet pregnant, lines we may compare the more elaborate statement of the same thought in the following passage from the fourth book of "The Excursion." The argument, as such, is of course invalidated by the fact that its basis is a mere illusion. But this for the moment does not matter.

I have seen
A curious child, who dwelt upon a tract
Of inland ground, applying to his ear

The convolutions of a smooth-lipped shell ;
To which, in silence hushed, his very soul
Listened intensely ; and his countenance soon
Brightened with joy ; for from within were heard
Murmurings, whereby the monitor expressed
Mysterious union with its native sea.
Even such a shell the universe itself
Is to the ear of Faith ; and there are times,
I doubt not, when to you it doth impart
Authentic tidings of invisible things ;
Of ebb and flow, and ever-during power ;
And central peace, subsisting at the heart
Of endless agitation.   Here you stand,
Adore, and worship, when you know it not ;
Pious beyond the intention of your thought ;
Devout above the meaning of your will.

Now for Wordsworth it is because of the
essential kinship between the spiritual faculty
in man and the indwelling soul of the universe
—because " the external World " and the Mind
are " exquisitely " fitted each to the other [1]—
that communion with nature is possible, and
that through such communion we find, as Mr.
Myers has put it, " an opening, if indeed there
be any opening, into the transcendent world."
To grasp this point is to have the key to Wordsworth's entire interpretation of nature ;   to
miss it, is to miss everything that is most
characteristic in that interpretation.   But, as it
is further necessary to realize, spiritual communion with nature is possible only on condition

[1] " The Excursion," Introduction, 62–71.

83

that we go to nature in the right mood—the mood, not of analysis and speculation, but of receptivity and deep religious contemplation. This is the " serene and blessed mood " of the Tintern Abbey " Lines "—the mood of mystical rapture in which the burden of thought is lifted from us and the power is granted to us to see into the very " life of things." One moment of such inner illumination, as we have already found the poet telling his sister, " may give us more than years of toiling reason."

We are now prepared to understand Wordsworth's famous thesis that nature is the best and truest of all teachers. This thesis fills a very large place in his poetry. It is succinctly and clearly set forth in two short poems, first published among the " Lyrical Ballads." Note should be taken of the stress once again laid upon the initial need of a right relationship with nature in our intercourse with her—of " a wise passiveness " in the one poem, and of " a heart that watches and receives " in the other.

EXPOSTULATION AND REPLY

" Why, William, on that old grey stone,
Thus for the length of half a day,
Why, William, sit you thus alone,
And dream your time away ?

" Where are your books ?—that light bequeathed
To Beings else forlorn and blind !
Up ! up ! and drink the spirit breathed
From dead men to their kind.

WORDSWORTH & HIS POETRY

" You look round on your Mother Earth,
As if she for no purpose bore you ;
As if you were her first-born birth,
And none had lived before you ! "

One morning thus, by Esthwaite lake,
When life was sweet, I knew not why,
To me my good friend Matthew spake,
And thus I made reply :

" The eye—it cannot choose but see ;
We cannot bid the ear be still ;
Our bodies feel, where'er they be,
Against or with our will.

" Nor less I deem that there are Powers
Which of themselves our minds impress ;
That we can feed this mind of ours
In a wise passiveness.

" Think you, 'mid all this mighty sum
Of things for ever speaking,
That nothing of itself will come,
But we must still be seeking ?

"—Then ask not wherefore, here, alone,
Conversing as I may,
I sit upon this old grey stone,
And dream my time away."

THE TABLES TURNED

Up ! up ! my Friend, and quit your books ;
Or surely you'll grow double :
Up ! up ! my Friend, and clear your looks ;
Why all this toil and trouble ?

WORDSWORTH & HIS POETRY

The sun, above the mountain's head,
A freshening lustre mellow
Through all the long green fields has spread,
His first sweet evening yellow.

Books ! 'tis a dull and endless strife :
Come, hear the woodland linnet,
How sweet his music ! on my life,
There's more of wisdom in it.

And hark ! how blithe the throstle sings !
He, too, is no mean preacher :
Come forth into the light of things,
Let Nature be your teacher.

She has a world of ready wealth,
Our minds and hearts to bless—
Spontaneous wisdom breathed by health,
Truth breathed by cheerfulness.

One impulse from a vernal wood
May teach you more of man,
Of moral evil and of good,
Than all the sages can.

Sweet is the lore which Nature brings ;
Our meddling intellect
Mis-shapes the beauteous forms of things :—
We murder to dissect.

Enough of Science and of Art ;
Close up those barren leaves ;
Come forth, and bring with you a heart
That watches and receives.

These poems undoubtedly contain high doctrine, and critics have not been wanting who

have accused Wordsworth of talking extravagance if not downright nonsense in them. Thus even Lord Morley dismisses impatiently the particular philosophy of which they are the vehicle : " no impulse from a vernal wood," he declares, " can teach us anything at all of moral evil and of good." But before we charge Wordsworth with absurdity it will be well to make sure that we really understand his position. Though his recoil from mere bookishness manifestly prompted him to a too emphatic and over-fanciful expression, I do not think he meant that nature teaches better than books the things which books teach. He meant that if we go to nature in the right mood, and throw ourselves open to her benign influences, we shall gain through communion with her more moral energy and more spiritual insight than we can ever get from all the philosophies of the schools, and that through such energy and insight we shall obtain a clearer vision of good and evil than mere knowledge will ever afford. This indeed may not correspond with the experience of the average man. But it did correspond with Wordsworth's, and for that reason we must at least treat it with respect.

There is, however, another criticism which may more justly be made upon Wordsworth's nature-poetry. It is that the view of nature which he presents is uniformly one-sided. Nature in his interpretation is always benignant. He dwells invariably upon its beauty, its harmony, its peace. Of its indifference and cruelty

he sees nothing. " All which we behold " is
for him " full of blessings." Nature never
brings to him, as it brought to Tennyson, " evil
dreams " ; he never realizes that it is " red in
tooth and claw with ravine." This incom-
pleteness of vision is at times a perverting factor
in his thought, for it leads him to a false
judgment of the relationship of nature and
humanity ; as when, in a poem recently
quoted, he finds in " Nature's holy plan "—a
plan which from the minutest beginnings of
life upward throughout its entire scale involves
wholesale and endless destruction—a condemnation of the barbarities of man. In our reading
of Wordsworth allowance must always be made
for the fallacy which thus runs through much
of his poetry. Yet that fallacy itself throws a
wonderful light upon his character. Nature is
to us what we are to nature.

> O Lady ! we receive but what we give,
> And in our life alone does Nature live :
> Ours is her wedding-garment, ours her shroud !
>   And would we aught behold, of higher worth,
> Than that inanimate cold world allowed
>   To the poor loveless ever-anxious crowd,
>   Ah ! from the soul itself must issue forth
>   A light, a glory, a fair luminous cloud
>   Enveloping the Earth—
>   And from the soul itself must there be sent
>   A sweet and potent voice, of its own birth,
>   Of all sweet sounds the life and element ! [1]

Byron, being Byron, saw nature in the tumult

[1] Coleridge : " Ode to Dejection."

of revolt. Wordsworth, being Wordsworth, found
in nature what he sought—the peace which was
in his own soul.

IX

ON September 14, 1798, a few days after the
publication of "Lyrical Ballads,"
Wordsworth, Dorothy, and Coleridge
left London for Germany ; Mrs. Coleridge being
left behind at Nether Stowey. At Hamburg,
where they met Klopstock, they passed some
time pleasantly enough. Then they parted
company ; Coleridge going on to Ratzeburg,
where amongst other things he proposed to
collect materials for a life of Lessing (never of
course to be written or even begun) ; the
Wordsworths settling in "the romantic imperial town of Goslar," where they took
lodgings over a draper's shop. There they
remained till the spring of 1799, but their visit,
to which they had looked forward with the
keenest pleasure, proved a great disappointment.
Goslar was desperately dull ; they had little
society and made few acquaintances ; living
was much dearer than they had anticipated ;
and the winter was of such exceptional severity
that the people of the house fully expected the
poet to be frozen to death in his unceiled
bedroom.[1] It was on the whole a dreary time
for both of them. But Wordsworth was not
inactive, though it is significant that he was

[1] See the lines "Written in Germany on One of the Coldest Days of the Century."

89

generally inspired by reminiscence (as in "Nutting," which belongs to this period), and not by the life about him. He now began "The Prelude" and wrote two very distinctive narrative poems, "Lucy Gray" and "Ruth." Regarding the former, which I shall here quote, Wordsworth said : "The way in which the incident was treated and the spiritualizing of the character might furnish hints for contrasting the imaginative influences which I have endeavoured to throw over common life with Crabbe's matter-of-fact style of treating subjects of the same kind." It must always be remembered that it was part of Wordsworth's aim to deal faithfully with reality without allowing fidelity to pass into the hard literalism of Crabbe. The passage previously quoted from the preface to the second edition of "Lyrical Ballads," with its reference to the "colouring of imagination" which he sought to throw over his themes, has already made this clear ; while Coleridge's account of the "Lyrical Ballads" touches, it will be remembered, upon the same point.

LUCY GRAY

Oft I had heard of Lucy Gray:
And, when I crossed the wild,
I chanced to see at break of day
The solitary child.

No mate, no comrade Lucy knew ;
She dwelt on a wide moor,
—The sweetest thing that ever grew
Beside a human door !

You yet may spy the fawn at play,
The hare upon the green ;
But the sweet face of Lucy Gray
Will never more be seen.

" To-night will be a stormy night—
You to the town must go ;
And take a lantern, Child, to light
Your mother through the snow."

" That, Father ! will I gladly do :
'Tis scarcely afternoon—
The minster-clock has just struck two,
And yonder is the moon ! "

At this the Father raised his hook,
And snapped a faggot-band ;
He plied his work ;—and Lucy took
The lantern in her hand.

Not blither is the mountain roe :
With many a wanton stroke
Her feet disperse the powdery snow,
That rises up like smoke.

The storm came on before its time :
She wandered up and down ;
And many a hill did Lucy climb :
But never reached the town.

The wretched parents all that night
Went shouting far and wide ;
But there was neither sound nor sight
To serve them for a guide.

At day-break on a hill they stood
That overlooked the moor ;
And thence they saw the bridge of wood,
A furlong from their door.

They wept—and, turning homeward, cried,
" In heaven we all shall meet ; "
—When in the snow the mother spied
The print of Lucy's feet.

Then downwards from the steep hill's edge
They tracked the footmarks small ;
And through the broken hawthorn hedge,
And by the long stone-wall ;

And then an open field they crossed :
The marks were still the same ;
They tracked them on, nor ever lost ;
And to the bridge they came.

They followed from the snowy bank
Those footmarks, one by one,
Into the middle of the plank ;
And further there were none !

—Yet some maintain that to this day
She is a living child ;
That you may see sweet Lucy Gray
Upon the lonesome wild.

O'er rough and smooth she trips along,
And never looks behind ;
And sings a solitary song
That whistles in the wind.

WORDSWORTH & HIS POETRY

To this Goslar period also belongs the group of exquisite lyrics, written early in 1799, which we know collectively as the " Lucy " poems. The genesis of these poems remains a mystery. Habitually garrulous about everything connected with his work, Wordsworth has told us nothing about these, except that they were composed in Germany, and one of them— " Three years she grew "—in the Harz Forest. Nor is information regarding them forthcoming from any other quarter. Are they perhaps the memorial, as the poet's curious reticence might seem to hint, of an episode which he chose to keep secret ? Or were the emotional experiences portrayed merely fictitious ? Was there ever any original of Lucy ? Or was she only the creature of a tender fancy ? To these questions there is no certain answer. This much alone is beyond dispute, that they have a delicate fragrance which is peculiarly their own, and a note of passion which makes them unique among Wordsworth's works. Their own restraint is of course remarkable, and the note of passion in them is manifestly very subdued. Yet it is in reading them, perhaps, that we can best understand a surprising remark which the poet once made to Aubrey de Vere. Asked by that friend why he had not written more love-poems, he replied : " Had I been a writer of love-poetry it would have been natural to me to write it with a degree of warmth which could hardly have been approved by my principles."

Strange fits of passion have I known :
And I will dare to tell,
But in the Lover's ear alone,
What once to me befell.

When she I loved looked every day
Fresh as a rose in June,
I to her cottage bent my way,
Beneath an evening-moon.

Upon the moon I fixed my eye,
All over the wide lea ;
With quickening pace my horse drew nigh
Those paths so dear to me.

And now we reached the orchard-plot ;
And, as we climbed the hill,
The sinking moon to Lucy's cot
Came near, and nearer still.

In one of those sweet dreams I slept,
Kind Nature's gentlest boon !
And all the while my eyes I kept
On the descending moon.

My horse moved on ; hoof after hoof
He raised, and never stopped :
When down behind the cottage roof,
At once, the bright moon dropped.

What fond and wayward thoughts will slide
Into a Lover's head !
" O mercy ! " to myself I cried,
" If Lucy should be dead ! "

. . .

WORDSWORTH & HIS POETRY

She dwelt among the untrodden ways
  Beside the springs of Dove,
A Maid whom there were none to praise
  And very few to love :

A violet by a mossy stone
  Half hidden from the eye !
—Fair as a star, when only one
  Is shining in the sky.

She lived unknown, and few could know
  When Lucy ceased to be ;
But she is in her grave, and, oh,
  The difference to me !

          .   .   .

I travelled among unknown men,
  In lands beyond the sea ;
Nor, England ! did I know till then
  What love I bore to thee.

'Tis past, that melancholy dream !
  Nor will I quit thy shore
A second time ; for still I seem
  To love thee more and more.

Among thy mountains did I feel
  The joy of my desire ;
And she I cherished turned her wheel
  Beside an English fire.

Thy mornings showed, thy nights concealed
  The bowers where Lucy played ;
And thine too is the last green field
  That Lucy's eyes surveyed.

          .   .   .

Three years she grew in sun and shower,
Then Nature said, " A lovelier flower
On earth was never sown ;
This Child I to myself will take ;
She shall be mine, and I will make
A Lady of my own.

" Myself will to my darling be
Both law and impulse : and with me
The Girl, in rock and plain,
In earth and heaven, in glade and bower,
Shall feel an overseeing power
To kindle or restrain.

" She shall be sportive as the fawn
That wild with glee across the lawn,
Or up the mountain springs ;
And her's shall be the breathing balm,
And her's the silence and the calm
Of mute insensate things.

" The floating clouds their state shall lend
To her ; for her the willow bend ;
Nor shall she fail to see
Even in the motions of the Storm
Grace that shall mould the Maiden's form
By silent sympathy.

" The stars of midnight shall be dear
To her ; and she shall lean her ear
In many a secret place
Where rivulets dance their wayward round,
And beauty born of murmuring sound
Shall pass into her face.

" And vital feelings of delight
Shall rear her form to stately height,
Her virgin bosom swell ;
Such thoughts to Lucy I will give
While she and I together live
Here in this happy dell.''

Thus Nature spake—The work was done—
How soon my Lucy's race was run !
She died, and left to me
This heath, this calm, and quiet scene ;
The memory of what has been,
And never more will be.

.   .   .

A slumber did my spirit seal ;
    I had no human fears :
She seemed a thing that could not feel
    The touch of earthly years.

No motion has she now, no force ;
    She neither hears nor sees ;
Rolled round in earth's diurnal course,
    With rocks, and stones, and trees.

Returning to England in April, brother and
sister spent some time in a round of visits to
relatives. Then in September, Coleridge, now
back from Germany, and as erratic as ever,
joined Wordsworth and his sailor-brother John
in a tour of the Lakes. During that tour
Wordsworth saw at Town-End, Grasmere, a
vacant cottage which took his fancy. Arrangements for tenancy were soon completed, and he
and Dorothy entered into possession of their

G

new home on December 20, 1799. He has
described their arrival in the hard winter
weather :

Stern was the face of nature ; we rejoiced
In that stern countenance, for our souls thence drew
A feeling of their strength.   The naked trees,
The icy brooks, as on we passed, appeared
To question us.   "Whence come ye, to what end ?"
They seemed to say, "What would ye," said the shower,
"Wild Wanderers, whither through my dark do-
     main ?"
The sunbeam said, "Be happy." When this vale
We entered, bright and solemn was the sky
That faced us with a passionate welcoming,
And led us to our threshold.   Daylight failed
Insensibly, and round us gently fell
Composing darkness, with a quiet load
Of full contentment, in a little shed
Disturbed, uneasy in itself as seemed,
And wondering at its new inhabitants.
It loves us now, this Vale so beautiful
Begins to love us ! by a sullen storm,
Two months unwearied of severest storm,
It put the temper of our minds to proof,
And found us faithful through the gloom, and heard
The poet mutter his prelusive songs
With cheerful heart, an unknown voice of joy
Among the silence of the woods and hills.[1]

Dove Cottage, as their dwelling was called,
stands close to the road, with a garden and
orchard at the back, and behind these a steep
hill.   A little " semi-vestibule " opens directly

[1] "The Recluse."

on the living-room, which De Quincey described
as " an oblong square, not above eight and a
half feet high, sixteen feet long, and twelve
broad ; very prettily wainscoted from the floor
to the ceiling with dark polished oak, slightly
embellished with carving. One window there
was—a perfect and unpretending cottage window, with little diamond panes, embowered at
every season of the year with roses ; and in
the summer and autumn with a profusion of
jasmine and other fragrant shrubs. From the
exuberant luxuriance of the vegetation around
it, and from the dark hue of the wainscoting,
this window, though tolerably large, did not
furnish a very powerful light." On the ground
floor were the kitchen and Dorothy's bedroom ;
on the floor above, a little drawing-room over
the living-room, and Wordsworth's bedroom
over his sister's. The drawing-room was also
Wordsworth's library. " The two or three
hundred volumes," writes De Quincey, " occu-
pied a little, homely, painted bookcase, fixed
into one of two shallow recesses, formed on each
side of the fireplace by the projection of the
chimney. . . . They were ill-bound, or not
bound at all—in boards, sometimes in tatters ;
many were imperfect as to the number of
volumes, mutilated as to the number of pages ;
sometimes, where it seemed worth while, the
defects being supplied by manuscript ; sometimes not." It is evident, De Quincey con-
tinues, that the owner of these books must
have had " independent sources of enjoyment

to fill up the major part of his time." He was not indeed a bookman at all, in the sense in which his friend Southey, for example, was a bookman; "Books," he once said of Southey, "were in fact his *passion;* and *wandering,* I can with truth affirm, was mine." "Nine-tenths of my verses," he declared towards the end of his life, "have been murmured out in the open air. One day a stranger, having walked round the garden and grounds of Rydal Mount, asked one of the female servants, who happened to be at the door, permission to see her master's study. 'This,' said she, leading him forward, 'is my master's library, where he keeps his books, but his study is out of doors.' After a long absence from home it has more than once happened that some one of my cottage neighbours . . . has said, 'Well, there he is! we are glad to hear him *booing* about again.'"[1]

A few months after the settlement at Dove Cottage, Wordsworth was busy with a second edition of "Lyrical Ballads," in two volumes, with the famous polemical preface already referred to. This, though always spoken of as the edition of 1800, was actually published in January 1801, and was followed by a third edition in 1802 and a fourth in 1805. Perhaps the most important new poem in the enlarged collection is the one entitled "Michael," on the whole the finest example of Wordsworth's narrative poetry of humble life. He called it

Cp. "and heard the poet mutter his prelusive songs" in the passage just quoted from "The Recluse."

a " pastoral poem," thus challenging comparison with the conventional pastoralism, or hopelessly unreal treatment of shepherds and the country, which had long been a pernicious tradition in literature. The story itself, he explains, was the first of those " domestic tales " of his native region which had interested him even as a boy. " Homely and rude " he admits it to be ; yet he proposes to tell it " for the delight of a few natural hearts," and in the firm conviction that the emotions may be stirred without that " outrageous stimulation " by sensational incident against which it was in part the object of his preface to protest. " I have attempted," he wrote to his friend Thomas Poole, " to give a picture of a man of strong mind and lively sensibility, agitated by two of the most powerful affections of the human heart—the parental affection and the love of property, *landed* property, including the feelings of inheritance, home, and personal and family independence." Michael himself, as he told Charles James Fox, is in fact a kind of type of those " statesmen," or "independent proprietors of land," who " are now almost confined to the north of England " and " whose little tract of land serves as a kind of rallying point for their domestic feelings, as a tablet upon which they are written, which makes them objects of memory in a thousand instances, when they would otherwise be forgotten." This local feature in the poem must not be forgotten in the reading of it.

MICHAEL

If from the public way you turn your steps
Up the tumultuous brook of Greenhead Ghyll,
You will suppose that with an upright path
Your feet must struggle ; in such bold ascent
The pastoral mountains front you, face to face.
But, courage ! for around that boisterous brook
The mountains have all opened out themselves,
And made a hidden valley of their own.
No habitation can be seen ; but they
Who journey thither find themselves alone
With a few sheep, with rocks and stones, and kites
That overhead are sailing in the sky.
It is in truth an utter solitude ;
Nor should I have made mention of this Dell
But for one object which you might pass by,
Might see and notice not.   Beside the brook
Appears a straggling heap of unhewn stones !
And to that simple object appertains
A story—unenriched with strange events,
Yet not unfit, I deem, for the fireside,
Or for the summer shade.   It was the first
Of those domestic tales that spake to me
Of shepherds, dwellers in the valleys, men
Whom I already loved ; not verily
For their own sakes, but for the fields and hills
Where was their occupation and abode.
And hence this Tale, while I was yet a Boy
Careless of books, yet having felt the power
Of Nature, by the gentle agency
Of natural objects, led me on to feel
For passions that were not my own, and think
(At random and imperfectly indeed)
On man, the heart of man, and human life.

Therefore, although it be a history
Homely and rude, I will relate the same
For the delight of a few natural hearts ;
And, with yet fonder feeling, for the sake
Of youthful Poets, who among these hills
Will be my second self when I am gone.

   Upon the forest-side in Grasmere Vale
There dwelt a Shepherd, Michael was his name ;
An old man, stout of heart, and strong of limb.
His bodily frame had been from youth to age
Of an unusual strength : his mind was keen,
Intense, and frugal, apt for all affairs,
And in his shepherd's calling he was prompt
And watchful more than ordinary men.
Hence had he learned the meaning of all winds,
Of blasts of every tone ; and, oftentimes,
When others heeded not, he heard the South
Make subterraneous music, like the noise
Of bagpipers on distant Highland hills.
The Shepherd, at such warning, of his flock
Bethought him, and he to himself would say,
" The winds are now devising work for me ! "
And, truly, at all times, that storm, that drives
The traveller to a shelter, summoned him
Up to the mountains : he had been alone
Amid the heart of many thousand mists,
That came to him, and left him, on the heights.
So lived he till his eightieth year was past.
And grossly that man errs, who should suppose
That the green valleys, and the streams and rocks,
Were things indifferent to the Shepherd's thoughts.
Fields, where with cheerful spirits he had breathed
The common air ; hills, which with vigorous step
He had so often climbed ; which had impressed
So many incidents upon his mind

Of hardship, skill or courage, joy or fear ;
Which, like a book, preserved the memory
Of the dumb animals, whom he had saved,
Had fed or sheltered, linking to such acts
The certainty of honourable gain ;
Those fields, those hills—what could they less ? had
    laid
Strong hold on his affections, were to him
A pleasurable feeling of blind love,
The pleasure which there is in life itself.
  His days had not been passed in singleness.
His Helpmate was a comely matron, old—
Though younger than himself full twenty years.
She was a woman of a stirring life,
Whose heart was in her house : two wheels she
    had
Of antique form ; this large, for spinning wool ;
That small, for flax ; and if one wheel had rest
It was because the other was at work.
The Pair had but one inmate in their house,
An only Child, who had been born to them
When Michael, telling o'er his years, began
To deem that he was old,—in shepherd's phrase,
With one foot in the grave. This only Son,
With two brave sheep-dogs tried in many a storm,
The one of an inestimable worth,
Made all their household. I may truly say,
That they were as a proverb in the vale
For endless industry. When day was gone,
And from their occupations out of doors
The Son and Father were come home, even then,
Their labour did not cease ; unless when all
Turned to the cleanly supper-board, and there,
Each with a mess of pottage and skimmed milk,
Sat round the basket piled with oaten cakes,

And their plain home-made cheese. Yet when the
  meal
Was ended, Luke (for so the Son was named)
And his old Father both betook themselves
To such convenient work as might employ
Their hands by the fireside ; perhaps to card
Wool for the Housewife's spindle, or repair
Some injury done to sickle, flail, or scythe,
Or other implement of house or field.
  Down from the ceiling, by the chimney's edge,
That in our ancient uncouth country style
With huge and black projection overbrowed
Large space beneath, as duly as the light
Of day grew dim the Housewife hung a lamp ;
An aged utensil, which had performed
Service beyond all others of its kind.
Early at evening did it burn—and late,
Surviving comrade of uncounted hours,
Which, going by from year to year, had found,
And left, the couple neither gay perhaps
Nor cheerful, yet with objects and with hopes,
Living a life of eager industry.
And now, when Luke had reached his eighteenth year,
There by the light of this old lamp they sate,
Father and Son, while far into the night
The Housewife plied her own peculiar work,
Making the cottage through the silent hours
Murmur as with the sound of summer flies.
This light was famous in its neighbourhood,
And was a public symbol of the life
That thrifty Pair had lived. For, as it chanced,
Their cottage on a plot of rising ground
Stood single, with large prospect, north and south,
High into Easedale, up to Dunmail-Raise,
And westward to the village near the lake ;

And from this constant light, so regular
And so far seen, the House itself, by all
Who dwelt within the limits of the vale,
Both old and young, was named *The Evening Star*.

Thus living on through such a length of years,
The Shepherd, if he loved himself, must needs
Have loved his Helpmate ; but to Michael's heart
This son of his old age was yet more dear—
Less from instinctive tenderness, the same
Fond spirit that blindly works in the blood of all—
Than that a child, more than all other gifts
That earth can offer to declining man,
Brings hope with it, and forward-looking thoughts,
And stirrings of inquietude, when they
By tendency of nature needs must fail.
Exceeding was the love he bare to him,
His heart and his heart's joy !   For oftentimes
Old Michael, while he was a babe in arms,
Had done him female service, not alone
For pastime and delight, as is the use
Of fathers, but with patient mind enforced
To acts of tenderness ; and he had rocked
His cradle, as with a woman's gentle hand.

And, in a later time, ere yet the Boy
Had put on boy's attire, did Michael love,
Albeit of a stern unbending mind,
To have the Young-one in his sight, when he
Wrought in the field, or on his shepherd's stool
Sate with a fettered sheep before him stretched
Under the large old oak, that near his door
Stood single, and, from matchless depth of shade,
Chosen for the Shearer's covert from the sun,
Thence in our rustic dialect was called
The *Clipping Tree,* a name which yet it bears.
There, while they two were sitting in the shade,

With others round them, earnest all and blithe,
Would Michael exercise his heart with looks
Of fond correction and reproof bestowed
Upon the Child, if he disturbed the sheep
By catching at their legs, or with his shouts
Scared them, while they lay still beneath the shears.

   And when by Heaven's good grace the boy grew up
A healthy Lad, and carried in his cheek
Two steady roses that were five years old ;
Then Michael from a winter coppice cut
With his own hand a sapling, which he hooped
With iron, making it throughout in all
Due requisites a perfect shepherd's staff,
And gave it to the Boy ; wherewith equipt
He as a watchman oftentimes was placed
At gate or gap, to stem or turn the flock ;
And, to his office prematurely called,
There stood the urchin, as you will divine,
Something between a hindrance and a help ;
And for this cause not always, I believe,
Receiving from his Father hire of praise ;
Though nought was left undone which staff, or voice,
Or looks, or threatening gestures, could perform.

   But soon as Luke, full ten years old, could stand
Against the mountain blasts ; and to the heights,
Not fearing toil, nor length of weary ways,
He with his Father daily went, and they
Were as companions, why should I relate
That objects which the Shepherd loved before
Were dearer now ? that from the Boy there came
Feelings and emanations—things which were
Light to the sun and music to the wind ;
And that the old Man's heart seemed born again ?

   Thus in his Father's sight the Boy grew up :
And now, when he had reached his eighteenth year,

He was his comfort and his daily hope.
  While in this sort the simple household lived
From day to day, to Michael's ear there came
Distressful tidings.   Long before the time
Of which I speak, the Shepherd had been bound
In surety for his brother's son, a man
Of an industrious life, and ample means ;
But unforeseen misfortunes suddenly
Had prest upon him ; and old Michael now
Was summoned to discharge the forfeiture,
A grievous penalty, but little less
Than half his substance.   This unlooked-for claim,
At the first hearing, for a moment took
More hope out of his life than he supposed
That any old man ever could have lost.
As soon as he had armed himself with strength
To look his trouble in the face, it seemed
The Shepherd's sole resource to sell at once
A portion of his patrimonial fields.
Such was his first resolve ; he thought again,
And his heart failed him.   " Isabel," said he,
Two evenings after he had heard the news,
" I have been toiling more than seventy years,
And in the open sunshine of God's love
Have we all lived ; yet if these fields of ours
Should pass into a stranger's hand, I think
That I could not lie quiet in my grave.
Our lot is a hard lot ; the sun himself
Has scarcely been more diligent than I ;
And I have lived to be a fool at last
To my own family.   An evil man
That was, and made an evil choice, if he
Were false to us ; and if he were not false,
There are ten thousand to whom loss like this
Had been no sorrow.   I forgive him ;—but

'Twere better to be dumb than to talk thus.
When I began, my purpose was to speak
Of remedies and of a cheerful hope.
Our Luke shall leave us, Isabel ; the land
Shall not go from us, and it shall be free ;
He shall possess it, free as is the wind
That passes over it.   We have, thou know'st,
Another kinsman—he will be our friend
In this distress.   He is a prosperous man,
Thriving in trade—and Luke to him shall go,
And with his kinsman's help and his own thrift
He quickly will repair this loss, and then
He may return to us.   If here he stay,
What can be done ?   Where every one is poor,
What can be gained ? "
                    At this the old Man paused,
And Isabel sat silent, for her mind
Was busy, looking back into past times.
There's Richard Bateman, thought she to herself,
He was a parish-boy—at the church-door
They made a gathering for him, shillings, pence
And halfpennies, wherewith the neighbours bought
A basket, which they filled with pedlar's wares ;
And, with this basket on his arm, the lad
Went up to London, found a master there,
Who, out of many, chose the trusty boy
To go and overlook his merchandise
Beyond the seas ; where he grew wondrous rich,
And left estates and monies to the poor.
And, at his birth-place, built a chapel, floored
With marble which he sent from foreign lands.
These thoughts, and many others of like sort,
Passed quickly through the mind of Isabel,
And her face brightened.   The old Man was glad,
And thus resumed :—" Well, Isabel ! this scheme

These two days, has been meat and drink to me.
Far more than we have lost is left us yet.
—We have enough—I wish indeed that I
Were younger ;—but this hope is a good hope.
—Make ready Luke's best garments, of the best
Buy for him more, and let us send him forth
To-morrow, or the next day, or to-night :
—If he *could* go, the Boy should go to-night."
  Here Michael ceased, and to the fields went forth
With a light heart. The Housewife for five days
Was restless morn and night, and all day long
Wrought on with her best fingers to prepare
Things needful for the journey of her son.
But Isabel was glad when Sunday came
To stop her in her work : for, when she lay
By Michael's side, she through the last two nights
Heard him, how he was troubled in his sleep :
And when they rose at morning she could see
That all his hopes were gone. That day at noon
She said to Luke, while they two by themselves
Were sitting at the door, " Thou must not go :
We have no other Child but thee to lose,
None to remember—do not go away,
For if thou leave thy Father he will die."
The Youth made answer with a jocund voice ;
And Isabel, when she had told her fears,
Recovered heart. That evening her best fare
Did she bring forth, and all together sat
Like happy people round a Christmas fire.
  With daylight Isabel resumed her work ;
And all the ensuing week the house appeared
As cheerful as a grove in Spring : at length
The expected letter from their kinsman came,
With kind assurances that he would do
His utmost for the welfare of the Boy;

To which, requests were added, that forthwith
He might be sent to him. Ten times or more
The letter was read over ; Isabel
Went forth to show it to the neighbours round ;
Nor was there at that time on English land
A prouder heart than Luke's. When Isabel
Had to her house returned, the old Man said,
" He shall depart to-morrow." To this word
The Housewife answered, talking much of things
Which, if at such short notice he should go,
Would surely be forgotten. But at length
She gave consent, and Michael was at ease.

  Near the tumultuous brook of Greenhead Ghyll,
In that deep valley, Michael had designed
To build a Sheepfold ; and, before he heard
The tidings of his melancholy loss,
For this same purpose he had gathered up
A heap of stones, which by the streamlet's edge
Lay thrown together, ready for the work.
With Luke that evening thitherward he walked :
And soon as they had reached the place he stopped,
And thus the old Man spake to him :—" My Son,
To-morrow thou wilt leave me : with full heart
I look upon thee, for thou art the same
That wert a promise to me ere thy birth,
And all thy life hast been my daily joy.
I will relate to thee some little part
Of our two histories ; 'twill do thee good
When thou art from me, even if I should touch
On things thou canst not know of.—After thou
First cam'st into the world—as oft befalls
To new-born infants—thou didst sleep away
Two days, and blessings from thy Father's tongue
Then fell upon thee. Day by day passed on,
And still I loved thee with increasing love.

Never to living ear came sweeter sounds
Than when I heard thee by our own fireside
First uttering, without words, a natural tune ;
While thou, a feeding babe, didst in thy joy
Sing at thy Mother's breast.   Month followed month,
And in the open fields my life was passed
And on the mountains ; else I think that thou
Hadst been brought up upon thy Father's knees.
But we were playmates, Luke : among these hills,
As well thou knowest, in us the old and young
Have played together, nor with me didst thou
Lack any pleasure which a boy can know.''
Luke had a manly heart ; but at these words
He sobbed aloud.   The old Man grasped his hand,
And said, '' Nay, do not take it so—I see
That these are things of which I need not speak.
—Even to the utmost I have been to thee
A kind and a good Father : and herein
I but repay a gift which I myself
Received at others' hands ; for, though now old
Beyond the common life of man, I still
Remember them who loved me in my youth.
Both of them sleep together : here they lived,
As all their Forefathers had done ; and when
At length their time was come, they were not loth
To give their bodies to the family mould.
I wished that thou should'st live the life they lived :
But, 'tis a long time to look back, my Son,
And see so little gain from threescore years.
These fields were burthened when they came to
    me ;
Till I was forty years of age, not more
Than half of my inheritance was mine.
I toiled and toiled ; God blessed me in my work,
And till these three weeks past the land was free.

—It looks as if it never could endure
Another Master.   Heaven forgive me, Luke,
If I judge ill for thee, but it seems good
That thou should'st go."
                              At this the old Man paused ;
Then, pointing to the stones near which they stood,
Thus, after a short silence, he resumed :
" This was a work for us ; and now, my Son,
It is a work for me.   But, lay one stone—
Here, lay it for me, Luke, with thine own hands.
Nay, Boy, be of good hope ;—we both may live
To see a better day.   At eighty-four
I still am strong and hale ;—do thou thy part ;
I will do mine.—I will begin again
With many tasks that were resigned to thee :
Up to the heights, and in among the storms,
Will I without thee go again, and do
All works which I was wont to do alone,
Before I knew thy face.—Heaven bless thee, Boy !
Thy heart these two weeks has been beating fast
With many hopes ; it should be so—yes—yes—
I knew that thou could'st never have a wish
To leave me, Luke : thou hast been bound to me
Only by links of love : when thou art gone,
What will be left to us !—But, I forget
My purposes.   Lay now the corner-stone,
As I requested ; and hereafter, Luke,
When thou art gone away, should evil men
Be thy companions, think of me, my Son,
And of this moment ; hither turn thy thoughts,
And God will strengthen thee : amid all fear
And all temptation, Luke, I pray that thou
May'st bear in mind the life thy Fathers lived,
Who, being innocent, did for that cause
Bestir them in good deeds.   Now, fare thee well—

When thou return'st, thou in this place wilt see
A work which is not here : a covenant
'Twill be between us ; but, whatever fate
Befall thee, I shall love thee to the last,
And bear thy memory with me to the grave."
   The Shepherd ended here ; and Luke stooped down,
And, as his Father had requested, laid
The first stone of the Sheepfold. At the sight
The old Man's grief broke from him ; to his heart
He pressed his Son, he kissèd him and wept ;
And to the house together they returned.
—Hushed was that House in peace, or seeming peace,
Ere the night fell :—with morrow's dawn the Boy
Began his journey, and when he had reached
The public way, he put on a bold face ;
And all the neighbours, as he passed their doors,
Came forth with wishes and with farewell prayers,
That followed him till he was out of sight.
   A good report did from their Kinsman come,
Of Luke and his well-doing : and the Boy
Wrote loving letters, full of wondrous news,
Which, as the Housewife phrased it, were throughout
" The prettiest letters that were ever seen."
Both parents read them with rejoicing hearts.
So, many months passed on : and once again
The Shepherd went about his daily work
With confident and cheerful thoughts ; and now
Sometimes when he could find a leisure hour
He to that valley took his way, and there
Wrought at the Sheepfold. Meantime Luke began
To slacken in his duty ; and, at length,
He in the dissolute city gave himself
To evil courses : ignominy and shame
Fell on him, so that he was driven at last
To seek a hiding-place beyond the seas.

There is a comfort in the strength of love ;
'Twill make a thing endurable, which else
Would overset the brain, or break the heart :
I have conversed with more than one who well
Remember the old Man, and what he was
Years after he had heard this heavy news.
His bodily frame had been from youth to age
Of an unusual strength.   Among the rocks
He went, and still looked up to sun and cloud,
And listened to the wind ; and, as before,
Performed all kinds of labour for his sheep,
And for the land, his small inheritance.
And to that hollow dell from time to time
Did he repair, to build the Fold of which
His flock had need.   'Tis not forgotten yet
The pity which was then in every heart
For the old Man—and 'tis believed by all
That many and many a day he thither went,
And never lifted up a single stone.
  There, by the Sheepfold, sometimes was he seen
Sitting alone, or with his faithful Dog,
Then old, beside him, lying at his feet.
The length of full seven years, from time to time,
He at the building of this Sheepfold wrought,
And left the work unfinished when he died.
Three years, or little more, did Isabel
Survive her Husband : at her death the estate
Was sold, and went into a stranger's hand.
The Cottage which was named the *Evening Star*
Is gone—the ploughshare has been through the ground
On which it stood ; great changes have been wrought
In all the neighbourhood :—yet the oak is left
That grew beside their door ; and the remains
Of the unfinished Sheepfold may be seen
Beside the boisterous brook of Greenhead Ghyll.

With this poem it is natural to associate one written some two years later, in which the same deep sympathy is shown with the lives and sufferings of the poor. In "Resolution and Independence," however, the central interest lies, not in the narrative itself, but in the moral deduced, and that moral is distinctively Wordsworthian. That through faith and fortitude a man may lift himself above the influence of external circumstance was one of his cardinal thoughts, and it is very characteristic of him that this inspiring lesson should here be linked with a figure so obscure as that of the old leech-gatherer. His own account of the poem, contained in a letter to some friends, will be read with interest.

I will explain to you in prose my feelings in writing *that* poem. . . . I describe myself as having been exalted to the highest pitch of delight by the joyousness and beauty of nature ; and then as depressed, even in the midst of those beautiful objects, to the lowest dejection and despair. A young poet in the midst of the happiness of nature is described as overwhelmed by the thoughts of the miserable reverses which have befallen the happiest of men, *viz.* poets. I think of this till I am so deeply impressed with it that I consider the manner in which I was rescued from my dejection and despair almost as an interposition of Providence. A person reading the poem with feelings like mine will have been awed and controlled, expecting something spiritual or supernatural. What is brought forward ? A lonely place, "a pond by which an old man *was*, far from all house or home " ;[1] not *stood*, nor *sat*, but *was*,—the figure presented in the most naked simplicity possible. The feeling of spirituality or supernaturalness is again referred to as being strong in my mind in this passage. "How came he here ? " thought I, " or what can he be doing ? " I then described him, whether ill or well is not for me to judge with perfect confidence ; but this I *can* affirm, that though I believe God has given me a strong imagination, I cannot conceive a figure more impressive than that of an old man like this, the survivor of a wife and ten children, travelling alone among the mountains and all lonely places, carrying with him his own fortitude and the necessities which an unjust state of society has laid upon him.

RESOLUTION AND INDEPENDENCE

There was a roaring in the wind all night ;
The rain came heavily and fell in floods ;
But now the sun is rising calm and bright ;
The birds are singing in the distant woods ;
Over his own sweet voice the Stock-dove broods ;
The Jay makes answer as the Magpie chatters ;
And all the air is filled with pleasant noise of waters.

All things that love the sun are out of doors ;
The sky rejoices in the morning's birth ;
The grass is bright with rain-drops ;—on the moors
The hare is running races in her mirth ;
And with her feet she from the plashy earth
Raises a mist, that, glittering in the sun,
Runs with her all the way, wherever she doth run.

[1] The text was subsequently altered at this point, as will be seen.

WORDSWORTH & HIS POETRY

I was a Traveller then upon the moor,
I saw the hare that raced about with joy ;
I heard the woods and distant waters roar ;
Or heard them not, as happy as a boy :
The pleasant season did my heart employ :
My old remembrances went from me wholly ;
And all the ways of men, so vain and melancholy.

But, as it sometimes chanceth, from the might
Of joy in minds that can no further go,
As high as we have mounted in delight
In our dejection do we sink as low ;
To me that morning did it happen so ;
And fears and fancies thick upon me came ;
Dim sadness—and blind thoughts, I knew not, nor
    could name.

I heard the sky-lark warbling in the sky ;
And I bethought me of the playful hare :
Even such a happy Child of earth am I ;
Even as these blissful creatures do I fare ;
Far from the world I walk, and from all care ;
But there may come another day to me—
Solitude, pain of heart, distress, and poverty.

My whole life I have lived in pleasant thought,
As if life's business were a summer mood ;
As if all needful things would come unsought
To genial faith, still rich in genial good ;
But how can He expect that others should
Build for him, sow for him, and at his call
Love him, who for himself will take no heed at all ?

I thought of Chatterton, the marvellous Boy,
The sleepless Soul that perished in his pride ;
Of Him who walked in glory and in joy

WORDSWORTH & HIS POETRY

Following his plough, along the mountain-side :
By our own spirits are we deified :
We Poets in our youth begin in gladness ;
But thereof come in the end despondency and madness.

Now, whether it were by peculiar grace,
A leading from above, a something given,
Yet it befell, that, in this lonely place,
When I with these untoward thoughts had striven,
Beside a pool bare to the eye of heaven
I saw a Man before me unawares :
The oldest man he seemed that ever wore grey hairs.

As a huge stone is sometimes seen to lie
Couched on the bald top of an eminence ;
Wonder to all who do the same espy,
By what means it could thither come, and whence ;
So that it seems a thing endued with sense :
Like a sea-beast crawled forth, that on a shelf
Of rock or sand reposeth, there to sun itself ;

Such seemed this Man, not all alive nor dead,
Nor all asleep—in his extreme old age :
His body was bent double, feet and head
Coming together in life's pilgrimage ;
As if some dire constraint of pain, or rage
Of sickness felt by him in times long past,
A more than human weight upon his frame had cast.

Himself he propped, limbs, body, and pale face,
Upon a long grey staff of shaven wood :
And, still as I drew near with gentle pace,
Upon the margin of that moorish flood
Motionless as a cloud the old Man stood,
That heareth not the loud winds when they call
And moveth all together, if it move at all.

WORDSWORTH & HIS POETRY

At length, himself unsettling, he the pond
Stirred with his staff, and fixedly did look
Upon the muddy water, which he conned,
As if he had been reading in a book :
And now a stranger's privilege I took ;
And, drawing to his side, to him did say,
" This morning gives us promise of a glorious day."

A gentle answer did the old Man make,
In courteous speech which forth he slowly drew :
And him with further words I thus bespake,
" What occupation do you there pursue ?
This is a lonesome place for one like you."
Ere he replied, a flash of mild surprise
Broke from the sable orbs of his yet-vivid eyes,

His words came feebly, from a feeble chest,
But each in solemn order followed each,
With something of a lofty utterance drest—
Choice word and measured phrase, above the reach
Of ordinary men ; a stately speech ;
Such as grave Livers do in Scotland use,
Religious men, who give to God and man their dues.

He told, that to these waters he had come
To gather leeches, being old and poor :
Employment hazardous and wearisome !
And he had many hardships to endure :
From pond to pond he roamed, from moor to moor ;
Housing, with God's good help, by choice or chance,
And in this way he gained an honest maintenance.

The old Man still stood talking by my side ;
But now his voice to me was like a stream
Scarce heard ; nor word from word could I divide ;

And the whole body of the Man did seem
Like one whom I had met with in a dream ;
Or like a man from some far region sent,
To give me human strength, by apt admonishment.

My former thoughts returned : the fear that kills ;
And hope that is unwilling to be fed ;
Cold, pain, and labour, and all fleshly ills ;
And mighty Poets in their misery dead.
—Perplexed, and longing to be comforted,
My question eagerly did I renew,
" How is it that you live, and what is it you do ? "

He with a smile did then his words repeat ;
And said, that, gathering leeches, far and wide
He travelled ; stirring thus about his feet
The waters of the pools where they abide.
" Once I could meet with them on every side ;
But they have dwindled long by slow decay ;
Yet still I persevere, and find them where I may."

While he was talking thus, the lonely place,
The old Man's shape, and speech—all troubled me :
In my mind's eye I seemed to see him pace
About the weary moors continually,
Wandering about alone and silently.
While I these thoughts within myself pursued,
He, having made a pause, the same discourse renewed.

And soon with this he other matter blended,
Cheerfully uttered, with demeanour kind,
But stately in the main ; and when he ended,
I could have laughed myself to scorn to find
In that decrepit Man so firm a mind.
" God," said I, " be my help and stay secure ;
I'll think of the Leech-gatherer on the lonely moor ! "

WORDSWORTH & HIS POETRY

In 1801 Wordsworth began to use the sonnet. One afternoon his sister read to him some sonnets of Milton. Already acquainted with them as he was, he was then particularly struck by their " dignity, simplicity, and majestic harmony." He at once " took fire," and that same afternoon produced three sonnets—" the first I ever wrote except an irregular one at school."

The next year he and Dorothy spent a month's holiday in Calais. On July 31 they left London for Dover, and at a very early hour crossed Westminster Bridge. Here is an extract from Dorothy's " Journal " :—

Left London between five and six o'clock of the morning outside the Dover coach. A beautiful morning. The city, St. Paul's, with the river—a multitude of little boats, made a beautiful sight as we crossed Westminster Bridge ; the houses not over-hung by their clouds of smoke, and were hung out endlessly ; yet the sun shone so brightly, with such a pure light, that there was something like the purity of one of Nature's own grand spectacles.

Such was the impression which that early morning ride made upon one of the two travellers. The impression which it made upon the other is to be found in the magnificent sonnet—one of Wordsworth's most perfect things—which was actually written on the roof of the coach, and afterwards underwent no verbal change.

122

WORDSWORTH & HIS POETRY

COMPOSED UPON WESTMINSTER BRIDGE

SEPTEMBER 3, 1802.[1]

Earth has not anything to show more fair :
Dull would he be of soul who could pass by
A sight so touching in its majesty :
This City now doth, like a garment, wear
The beauty of the morning ; silent, bare,
Ships, towers, domes, theatres, and temples lie
Open unto the fields, and to the sky ;
All bright and glittering in the smokeless air.
Never did sun more beautifully steep
In his first splendour, valley, rock, or hill ;
Ne'er saw I, never felt, a calm so deep !
The river glideth at his own sweet will :
Dear God ! the very houses seem asleep ;
And all that mighty heart is lying still !

Several sonnets were written during the stay
at Calais, among them one almost as fine as the
foregoing.

It is a beauteous evening, calm and free,
The holy time is quiet as a Nun
Breathless with adoration ; the broad sun
Is sinking down in its tranquillity ;
The gentleness of heaven broods o'er the Sea :
Listen ! the mighty Being is awake,
And doth with his eternal motion make
A sound like thunder—everlastingly.

---

[1] Wordsworth's date is now known to be incorrect. As Prof. Knight says, Wordsworth's memory was not always to be trusted in regard to dates.

Dear Child ! dear Girl ! that walkest with me here,[1]
If thou appear untouched by solemn thought,
Thy nature is not therefore less divine :
Thou liest in Abraham's bosom all the year ;
And worship'st at the Temple's inner shrine,
God being with thee when we know it not.

Wordsworth was the most prolific, and on the whole perhaps the greatest, of English sonnet-writers ; he produced upwards of 400 poems in this form ; and while many of these (including the 132 of the Ecclesiastical series and the 14 on the Punishment of Death) belong to the least inspired part of his output, his best work in this difficult field by reason of its volume no less than of its excellence entitles him to a position of pre-eminence. Undoubtedly the severe limitations of the form itself exercised a beneficial influence on his style. " In his larger poems his language is sometimes slovenly, and occasionally, as Sir Walter Scott said, he chooses to crawl on all-fours ; but this is rarely the case in the Sonnets . . . the language, like the thought, is that of a great master." [2] Two of his sonnets are sonnets on the sonnet, and these, though of later composition, may fittingly be given here.

Nuns fret not at their convent's narrow room ;
And hermits are contented with their cells ;
And students with their pensive citadels ;

[1] It is a question whether this refers to Dorothy, or, as seems more probable, to one of two companions of the Wordsworths, Annette and Caroline Vallon, the latter the natural daughter of Wordsworth, born in 1792, and the former the child's mother.

[2] J. Dennis, " English Sonnets," pp. 220, 221.

Maids at the wheel, the weaver at his loom,
Sit blithe and happy ; bees that soar for bloom,
High as the highest Peak of Furness-fells,
Will murmur by the hour in foxglove bells :
In truth the prison, unto which we doom
Ourselves, no prison is : and hence for me,
In sundry moods, 'twas pastime to be bound
Within the Sonnet's scanty plot of ground ;
Pleased if some Souls (for such there needs must be)
Who have felt the weight of too much liberty,
Should find brief solace there, as I have found.

Scorn not the Sonnet ; Critic, you have frowned,
Mindless of its just honours ; with this key
Shakspeare unlocked his heart ; the melody
Of this small lute gave ease to Petrarch's wound ;
A thousand times this pipe did Tasso sound ;
With it Camöens soothed an exile's grief ;
The Sonnet glittered a gay myrtle leaf
Amid the cypress with which Dante crowned
His visionary brow : a glow-worm lamp,
It cheered mild Spenser, called from Faeryland
To struggle through dark ways ; and, when a damp
Fell round the path of Milton, in his hand
The Thing became a trumpet ; whence he blew
Soul-animating strains—alas, too few !

Soon after the settlement at Dove Cottage
Wordsworth's financial position was much
improved by the repayment by the second Lord
Lonsdale of the sum long owing by his father
to the Wordsworth family, together with all
interest accruing in the meantime. This may
perhaps have had something to do with an

important step now taken by the poet. On their
return from Calais he and Dorothy stayed for a
month in London, and on October 4 he was
quietly married in Brompton Church, Yorks, to
Mary Hutchinson. He took her back to Dove
Cottage, where her coming made little outward
difference in the arrangements of the household,
and did not in the least disturb the relations of
brother and sister. Once more it was a case of
three people with one soul. One poem belonging to the early years of his married life has
already been quoted. To this I will now add
two sonnets of many years later—1841—which
are eloquent of the deep and quiet love which
remained unchanged by lapse of time. The
occasion was the painting of a portrait of Mrs.
Wordsworth by Miss Margaret Gillies, and
Wordsworth told his daughter that he " never
poured out anything more truly from the
heart." This we can well believe. The touching tenderness of the second sonnet must always
give it a high place in that rarer kind of love
poetry which deals, not with love's spring-
tide of youthful passion, but with its calm
autumnal beauty.

TO A PAINTER

All praise the Likeness by thy skill portrayed ;
But 'tis a fruitless task to paint for me,
Who, yielding not to changes Time has made,
By the habitual light of memory see
Eyes unbedimmed, see bloom that cannot fade,

And smiles that from their birth-place ne'er shall
    flee
Into the land where ghosts and phantoms be ;
And, seeing this, own nothing in its stead.
Couldst thou go back into far-distant years,
Or share with me, fond thought ! that inward eye,
Then, and then only, Painter ! could thy Art
The visual powers of Nature satisfy,
Which hold, whate'er to common sight appears,
Their sovereign empire in a faithful heart.

ON THE SAME SUBJECT

Though I beheld at first with blank surprise
This Work, I now have gazed on it so long
I see its truth with unreluctant eyes ;
O, my Belovèd ! I have done thee wrong,
Conscious of blessedness, but, whence it sprung,
Ever too heedless, as I now perceive :
Morn into noon did pass, noon into eve,
And the old day was welcome as the young,
As welcome, and as beautiful—in sooth
More beautiful, as being a thing more holy :
Thanks to thy virtues, to the eternal youth
Of all thy goodness, never melancholy ;
To thy large heart and humble mind, that cast
Into one vision, future, present, past.

127

X

IN June 1803 Wordsworth's first child, a son, was born, and on August 16 he set out for a tour in Scotland with Dorothy and Coleridge as his companions. Coleridge was, however, as Wordsworth said, " in bad spirits, and somewhat too much in love with his own dejection " ; he soon tired of the incessant rains, and at Loch Lomond gave up the expedition and started for Edinburgh, leaving brother and sister to go on together.

On the day of his departure, which was Sunday, August 28, as the friends were descending a hill towards the loch, they overtook two grey-plaided girls. " They answered us," writes Dorothy in her " Journal," " so sweetly that we were quite delighted, at the same time that they stared at us with an innocent look of wonder. I think I never heard the English language sound more sweetly than from the mouth of the elder of these girls, while she stood at the gate answering our inquiries, her face flushed with the rain ; her pronunciation was clear and distinct ; without difficulty ; yet slow, like that of a foreign speech." This elder girl, who was " exceedingly beautiful," made as strong an impression upon the two men of the party as upon Dorothy. Coleridge called her " a divine creature," and the memory of the meeting inspired Wordsworth, on his return home, to write the following poem.

TO A HIGHLAND GIRL

Sweet Highland Girl, a very shower
Of beauty is thy earthly dower !
Twice seven consenting years have shed
Their utmost bounty on thy head :
And these grey rocks ; that household lawn ;
Those trees, a veil just half withdrawn ;
This fall of water that doth make
A murmur near the silent lake ;
This little bay ; a quiet road
That holds in shelter thy Abode—
In truth together do ye seem
Like something fashioned in a dream ;
Such Forms as from their covert peep
When earthly cares are laid asleep !
But, O fair Creature ! in the light
Of common day, so heavenly bright,
I bless Thee, Vision as thou art,
I bless thee with a human heart ;
God shield thee to thy latest years !
Thee, neither know I, nor thy peers ;
And yet my eyes are filled with tears.
 With earnest feeling I shall pray
For thee when I am far away :
For never saw I mien, or face,
In which more plainly I could trace
Benignity and home-bred sense
Ripening in perfect innocence.
Here scattered, like a random seed,
Remote from men, Thou dost not need
The embarrassed look of shy distress,
And maidenly shamefacedness :
Thou wear'st upon thy forehead clear
The freedom of a Mountaineer :

WORDSWORTH & HIS POETRY

A face with gladness overspread !
Soft smiles, by human kindness bred !
And seemliness complete, that sways
Thy courtesies, about thee plays ;
With no restraint, but such as springs
From quick and eager visitings
Of thoughts that lie beyond the reach
Of thy few words of English speech :
A bondage sweetly brooked, a strife
That gives thy gestures grace and life
So have I, not unmoved in mind,
Seen birds of tempest-loving kind—
Thus beating up against the wind.

What hand but would a garland cull
For thee who art so beautiful ?
O happy pleasure ! here to dwell
Beside thee in some heathy dell ;
Adopt your homely ways, and dress,
A Shepherd, thou a Shepherdess !
But I could frame a wish for thee
More like a grave reality :
Thou art to me but as a wave
Of the wild sea ; and I would have
Some claim upon thee, if I could,
Though but of common neighbourhood.
What joy to hear thee, and to see !
Thy elder Brother I would be,
Thy Father—anything to thee !

Now thanks to Heaven ! that of its grace
Hath led me to this lonely place.
Joy have I had ; and going hence
I bear away my recompence.
In spots like these it is we prize
Our Memory, feel that she hath eyes :
Then, why should I be loth to stir ?

I feel this place was made for her ;
To give new pleasure like the past,
Continued long as life shall last.
Nor am I loth, though pleased at heart,
Sweet Highland Girl ! from thee to part :
For I, methinks, till I grow old,
As fair before me shall behold,
As I do now, the cabin small,
The lake, the bay, the waterfall ;
And Thee, the Spirit of them all !

"The sort of prophecy with which the verses conclude," Wordsworth told Miss Fenwick long afterwards, " has, through God's goodness, been realized, and now, approaching the close of my seventy-third year, I have a most vivid remembrance of her and the beautiful objects with which she was surrounded." She became for him indeed, it would seem, a kind of ideal type of womanly loveliness. He referred to her again in "The Three Cottage Girls" in his "Continental Memorials" seventeen years later ; and he even confessed—though such a confidence was perhaps scarcely judicious— that four lines (unidentified) originally composed as part of this Highland poem formed the germ of his verses to Mary Hutchinson, "She was a Phantom of Delight."

At Dumfries a visit was paid to the grave of Burns, then unmarked by any stone, and to the cottage where the poet died. This visit was commemorated in three poems in Burns's characteristic stanza-form, the first of which shall be here reproduced.

131

AT THE GRAVE OF BURNS

I shiver, Spirit fierce and bold,
At thought of what I now behold :
As vapours breathed from dungeons cold,
    Strike pleasure dead,
So sadness comes from out the mould
    Where Burns is laid.

And have I then thy bones so near,
And thou forbidden to appear ?
As if it were thyself that's here
    I shrink with pain ;
And both my wishes and my fear
    Alike are vain.

Off weight—nor press on weight !—away
Dark thoughts !—they came, but not to stay ;
With chastened feelings would I pay
    The tribute due
To him, and aught that hides his clay
    From mortal view.

Fresh as the flower, whose modest worth
He sang, his genius " glinted " forth,
Rose like a star that touching earth,
    For so it seems,
Doth glorify its humble birth
    With matchless beams.

The piercing eye, the thoughtful brow.
The struggling heart, where be they now ?—
Full soon the Aspirant of the plough,
    The prompt, the brave,
Slept, with the obscurest, in the low
    And silent grave.

WORDSWORTH & HIS POETRY

I mourned with thousands, but as one
More deeply grieved, for He was gone
Whose light I hailed when first it shone,
    And showed my youth
How Verse may build a princely throne
    On humble truth.

Alas ! where'er the current tends,
Regret pursues and with it blends,—
Huge Criffel's hoary top ascends
    By Skiddaw seen,—
Neighbours we were, and loving friends
    We might have been ;

True friends though diversely inclined ;
But heart with heart and mind with mind,
Where the main fibres are entwined,
    Through Nature's skill,
May even by contraries be joined
    More closely still.

The tear will start, and let it flow ;
Thou " poor Inhabitant below,"
At this dread moment—even so—
    Might we together
Have sate and talked where gowans blow,
    Or on wild heather.

What treasures would have then been placed
Within my reach ; of knowledge graced
By fancy what a rich repast !
    But why go on ?—
Oh ! spare to sweep, thou mournful blast,
    His grave grass-grown.

There, too, a Son, his joy and pride,
(Not three weeks past the Stripling died,)
Lies gathered to his Father's side,
    Soul-moving sight !
Yet one to which is not denied
    Some sad delight :

For *he* is safe, a quiet bed
Hath early found among the dead,
Harboured where none can be misled,
    Wronged, or distrest ;
And surely here it may be said
    That such are blest.

And oh for Thee, by pitying grace
Checked oft-times in a devious race,
May He who halloweth the place
    Where Man is laid
Receive thy Spirit in the embrace
    For which it prayed !

Sighing I turned away ; but ere
Night fell I heard, or seemed to hear,
Music that sorrow comes not near,
    A ritual hymn,
Chaunted in love that casts out fear
    By Seraphim.

Two other noteworthy poems are associated with this Scottish tour. The first of these, like the lines " To a Highland Girl," was the outcome of a chance meeting. One Sunday evening after sundown, brother and sister were walking along the shore of Lake Ketterine, when, as Dorothy records, they met " two neatly dressed women, without hats. . . . One of them said to us in a friendly soft tone of voice, ' What, are you stepping westward ? ' I cannot describe how affecting this simple expression was in that remote place, with the western sky in front, yet glowing with the departed sun. William wrote the following poem long after, in remembrance of his feelings and mine.''

STEPPING WESTWARD

" What, you are stepping westward?"—" Yea."
—'Twould be a *wildish* destiny,
If we, who thus together roam
In a strange Land, and far from home,
Were in this place the guests of Chance :
Yet who would stop, or fear to advance,
Though home or shelter he had none,
With such a sky to lead him on ?

The dewy ground was dark and cold ;
Behind, all gloomy to behold ;
And stepping westward seemed to be
A kind of *heavenly* destiny :
I liked the greeting ; 'twas a sound
Of something without place or bound ;
And seemed to give me spiritual right
To travel through that region bright.

The voice was soft, and she who spake
Was walking by her native lake :
The salutation had to me
The very sound of courtesy :
Its power was felt ; and while my eye
Was fixed upon the glowing Sky,

135

The echo of the voice enwrought
A human sweetness with the thought
Of travelling through the world that lay
Before me in my endless way.

The second of the two poems in question was inspired in part by his own experience, in part by that of another. The sight of the reapers in the harvest fields through which the tourists passed recalled to Wordsworth's mind "a beautiful sentence in a MS. 'Tour in Scotland' written by a friend, the last line being taken from it *verbatim*." The reference is to the following passage in Thomas Wilkinson's "Tours to the British Mountains" (published in 1824) : "Passed a female who was reaping alone ; she sang in Erse, as she bended over her sickle ; the sweetest human voice I ever heard ; her strains were tenderly melancholy, and felt delicious, long after they were heard no more." Such is the origin of "The Solitary Reaper," and there is perhaps no other poem of Wordsworth's which has so much verbal magic as this.

THE SOLITARY REAPER

Behold her, single in the field,
Yon solitary Highland Lass !
Reaping and singing by herself ;
Stop here, or gently pass !
Alone she cuts and binds the grain,
And sings a melancholy strain ;
O listen ! for the Vale profound
Is overflowing with the sound.

136

WORDSWORTH & HIS POETRY

No Nightingale did ever chaunt
More welcome notes to weary bands
Of travellers in some shady haunt,
Among Arabian sands :
A voice so thrilling ne'er was heard
In spring-time from the Cuckoo-bird,
Breaking the silence of the seas
Among the farthest Hebrides.

Will no one tell me what she sings ?—
Perhaps the plaintive numbers flow
For old, unhappy, far-off things,
And battles long ago :
Or is it some more humble lay,
Familiar matter of to-day ?
Some natural sorrow, loss, or pain,
That has been, and may be again ?

Whate'er the theme, the Maiden sang
As if her song could have no ending ;
I saw her singing at her work,
And o'er the sickle bending ;—
I listened, motionless and still ;
And, as I mounted up the hill
The music in my heart I bore,
Long after it was heard no more.

One great event which closed this Scottish
tour was Wordsworth's first meeting with
Scott, on whom he and his sister called at
Laswade so early in the morning that the
Border Minstrel was not yet out of bed. Scott
entertained them with his characteristic cor-
diality, and as he was himself bound for the
Jedburgh assizes, accompanied them south

through a region the romantic associations of which he was of all men the most competent to interpret. " My sister and I often talk of the happy days we spent in your company," wrote Wordsworth afterwards. " Such things do not often occur in life." The two poets parted at Hawick, and a couple of days later the Words- worths were once more at Dove Cottage. Dorothy's account of their return gives us so charming a glimpse of the little household that it must not be omitted : " Sunday, Sept. 25th, 1803. A beautiful autumnal day. Break- fasted at a public-house by the road-side ; dined at Threlkeld ; arrived at home between eight and nine o'clock, where we found Mary in perfect health, Joanna Hutchinson with her, and little John asleep in the clothes-basket by the fire."

XI

IN 1805 the shadow of a great sorrow fell suddenly across Wordsworth's placid life. His sailor-brother John, whom he loved with all the quiet intensity of his nature, was shipwrecked and drowned in the English Channel. " For myself," Wordsworth wrote in that hour of darkness, " I feel there is some- thing cut out of my life which cannot be restored. . . . I never wrote a line without thought of giving him pleasure. . . . But let me stop. I will not be cast down ; even if only for his sake I will not be dejected. I have much yet to do, and pray God to give me strength and power : his part of the agreement between us is brought to an end, mine remains ; and I hope when I shall be able to think of him with a calmer mind, that the remembrance of him dead will even animate me more than the joy which I had in him living.'' This is the '' deep distress '' which, he tells us, '' humanised '' his soul. He wrote some 'Elegiac Verses' in memory of his brother, but the note of sorrow is most finely struck, not in these, but rather in a poem belonging to the same period which ranks amongst the greatest of his productions, and which I here give in full. The Sir George Beaumont, to whom it introduces us, was a wealthy connoisseur whose friendship, as Mr. Myers has said, formed for many years the poet's '' closest link with the world of culture and art.'' He was not a great painter ; but the genuine feeling for nature shown in his landscapes made a strong appeal to Words-worth's sympathies.

ELEGIAC STANZAS

SUGGESTED BY A PICTURE OF PEELE CASTLE,[1] IN
A STORM, PAINTED BY SIR GEORGE BEAUMONT

I was thy neighbour once, thou rugged Pile !
Four summer weeks I dwelt in sight of thee :
I saw thee every day ; and all the while
Thy Form was sleeping on a glassy sea.

---

[1] Not apparently, as is commonly supposed, Peele Castle in the Isle of Man, but Piel Castle, near Barrow-in-Furness. See Prof. Knight's note in the Eversley edition of Wordsworth's '' Poetical Works,'' iii. 56, 57.

WORDSWORTH & HIS POETRY

So pure the sky, so quiet was the air !
So like, so very like, was day to day !
Whene'er I looked, thy Image still was there ;
It trembled, but it never passed away.

How perfect was the calm ! it seemed no sleep ;
No mood, which season takes away, or brings :
I could have fancied that the mighty Deep
Was even the gentlest of all gentle Things.

Ah ! then, if mine had been the Painter's hand,
To express what then I saw ; and add the gleam,
The light that never was, on sea or land,
The consecration, and the Poet's dream ;

I would have planted thee, thou hoary Pile,
Amid a world how different from this !
Beside a sea that could not cease to smile ;
On tranquil land, beneath a sky of bliss.

Thou shouldst have seemed a treasure-house divine
Of peaceful years ; a chronicle of heaven ;—
Of all the sunbeams that did ever shine
The very sweetest had to thee been given.

A Picture had it been of lasting ease,
Elysian quiet, without toil or strife ;
No motion but the moving tide, a breeze,
Or merely silent Nature's breathing life.

Such, in the fond illusion of my heart,
Such Picture would I at that time have made :
And seen the soul of truth in every part,
A stedfast peace that might not be betrayed.

140

WORDSWORTH & HIS POETRY

So once it would have been,—'tis so no more ;
I have submitted to a new control
A power is gone, which nothing can restore ;
A deep distress hath humanised my Soul.

Not for a moment could I now behold
A smiling sea, and be what I have been :
The feeling of my loss will ne'er be old ;
This, which I know, I speak with mind serene.

Then, Beaumont, Friend ! who would have been the
    Friend,
If he had lived, of Him whom I deplore,
This work of thine I blame not, but commend ;
This sea in anger, and that dismal shore.

O 'tis a passionate Work !—yet wise and well,
Well chosen is the spirit that is here ;
That Hulk which labours in the deadly swell,
This rueful sky, this pageantry of fear !

And this huge Castle, standing here sublime,
I love to see the look with which it braves,
Cased in the unfeeling armour of old time,
The lightning, the fierce wind, and trampling waves.

Farewell, farewell the heart that lives alone,
Housed in a dream, at distance from the Kind !
Such happiness, wherever it be known,
Is to be pitied ; for 'tis surely blind.

But welcome fortitude, and patient cheer,
And frequent sights of what is to be borne !
Such sights, or worse, as are before me here.—
Not without hope we suffer and we mourn.

WORDSWORTH & HIS POETRY

Another noble poem is connected with John's memory—the " Character of a Happy Warrior." Some of the features of this ideal portrait were admittedly derived from Nelson ; but Nelson's relations with Lady Hamilton made it impossible for Wordsworth " to connect his name with the poem as I could wish, or even to think of him with satisfaction in reference to the idea of what a warrior ought to be." This he subsequently stated in a note in which he further declared that "many elements of the character here portrayed were found in my brother John." As a study of ideal manhood, in which strength and tenderness, courage and purity are combined, this short poem is a masterpiece ; and there is, as has been well said, "a Roman majesty in its simple and weighty speech."

CHARACTER OF THE HAPPY WARRIOR

Who is the happy Warrior ?   Who is he
That every man in arms should wish to be ?
—It is the generous Spirit, who, when brought
Among the tasks of real life, hath wrought
Upon the plan that pleased his boyish thought :
Whose high endeavours are an inward light
That makes the path before him always bright :
Who, with a natural instinct to discern
What knowledge can perform, is diligent to learn ;
Abides by this resolve, and stops not there,
But makes his moral being his prime care ;
Who, doomed to go in company with Pain,
And Fear, and Bloodshed, miserable train !
Turns his necessity to glorious gain ;
In face of these doth exercise a power

Which is our human nature's highest dower ;
Controls them and subdues, transmutes, bereaves
Of their bad influence, and their good receives :
By objects, which might force the soul to abate
Her feeling, rendered more compassionate ;
Is placable—because occasions rise
So often that demand such sacrifice ;
More skilful in self-knowledge, even more pure,
As tempted more ; more able to endure,
As more exposed to suffering and distress ;
Thence, also, more alive to tenderness.
—'Tis he whose law is reason ; who depends
Upon that law as on the best of friends ;
Whence, in a state where men are tempted still
To evil for a guard against worse ill,
And what in quality or act is best
Doth seldom on a right foundation rest,
He labours good on good to fix, and owes
To virtue every triumph that he knows :
—Who, if he rise to station of command,
Rises by open means ; and there will stand
On honourable terms, or else retire,
And in himself possess his own desire ;
Who comprehends his trust, and to the same
Keeps faithful with a singleness of aim ;
And therefore does not stoop, nor lie in wait
For wealth, or honours, or for worldly state ;
Whom they must follow ; on whose head must fall,
Like showers of manna, if they come at all :
Whose powers shed round him in the common strife,
Or mild concerns of ordinary life,
A constant influence, a peculiar grace ;
But who, if he be called upon to face
Some awful moment to which Heaven has joined
Great issues, good or bad for human kind,

143

Is happy as a Lover ; and attired
With sudden brightness, like a Man inspired ;
And, through the heat of conflict, keeps the law
In calmness made, and sees what he foresaw ;
Or if an unexpected call succeed,
Come when it will, is equal to the need :
—He who, though thus endued as with a sense
And faculty for storm and turbulence,
Is yet a Soul whose master-bias leans
To homefelt pleasures and to gentle scenes ;
Sweet images ! which, wheresoe'er he be,
Are at his heart ; and such fidelity
It is his darling passion to approve ;
More brave for this, that he hath much to love :—
'Tis, finally, the Man, who, lifted high,
Conspicuous object in a Nation's eye,
Or left unthought-of in obscurity,—
Who, with a toward or untoward lot,
Prosperous or adverse, to his wish or not—
Plays, in the many games of life, that one
Where what he most doth value must be won :
Whom neither shape of danger can dismay,
Nor thought of tender happiness betray ;
Who, not content that former worth stand fast,
Looks forward, persevering to the last,
From well to better, daily self-surpast :
Who, whether praise of him must walk the earth
For ever, and to noble deeds give birth,
Or he must fall, to sleep without his fame,
And leave a dead unprofitable name—
Finds comfort in himself and in his cause ;
And, while the mortal mist is gathering, draws
His breath in confidence of Heaven's applause :
This is the happy Warrior ; this is He
That every Man in arms should wish to be.

WORDSWORTH & HIS POETRY

Before we close our record of the Dove Cottage period we have still to deal with the famous Immortality Ode, written according to Wordsworth's statement between 1803 and 1806, with an interval of " two years at least " between " the four first stanzas and the remaining part." In that interval, it is not inopportune to recall, he had lost his brother, and the tempering influences of sorrow are undoubtedly to be felt in the deepened tone of the concluding passages. It must be frankly admitted that there is an initial flaw in this great ode ; the Platonic idea from which it starts—that of the soul's pre-existence—has been justly censured as too fantastic to be made the basis of a philosophical poem ; and though Wordsworth himself protested against the literal interpretation of so " shadowy a notion," even its use as a symbol to represent the nearness of the child to nature and God may still be objected to on the ground that such a view of childhood is in flat contradiction to the facts of common experience. Yet as Wordsworth gives us poetry and not mere philosophy, inability to accept his data need not prevent us from enjoying the magnificent edifice which he rears upon them. Briefly stated, his argument seems to be this. The soul of man is divine ; it comes into this earthly life, not a blank (as Lockian empiricism had asserted), but bringing with it high spiritual instincts and powers. But the interests of the mundane and the temporal encroach upon it ; and the divine instincts are stifled. We must strive, therefore, to keep these instincts alive ; to maintain the continuity of spiritual life ; to translate into the reasoned convictions of manhood the child's innate and spontaneous faith. To do this we must live as much as possible among the deeper things of our own natures and in intimate communion with the divine soul of the universe. Then we shall rejoice that reminiscences of the distant past, faint and shadowy though they be, do in fact bear witness to the soul's divine origin and heritage and to its kinship with the eternal order of things.

ODE

INTIMATIONS OF IMMORTALITY FROM RECOLLECTIONS OF EARLY CHILDHOOD

There was a time when meadow, grove, and stream,
The earth, and every common sight,
  To me did seem
  Apparelled in celestial light,
The glory and the freshness of a dream.
It is not now as it hath been of yore ;—
  Turn wheresoe'er I may,
   By night or day,
The things which I have seen I now can see no more.

  The Rainbow comes and goes,
  And lovely is the Rose,
  The Moon doth with delight
Look round her when the heavens are bare,
  Waters on a starry night
  Are beautiful and fair ;

WORDSWORTH & HIS POETRY

The sunshine is a glorious birth ;
But yet I know, where'er I go,
That there hath past **away a** glory from the earth.

Now, while the birds thus sing a joyous song,
And while the young lambs bound
As to the tabor's sound,
To me alone there came a thought of grief :
A timely utterance gave that thought relief,
And I again am strong :
The cataracts blow their trumpets from the steep ;
No more shall grief of mine the season wrong ;
I hear the Echoes through the mountains throng,
The Winds come to me from the fields of sleep,
And all the earth is gay ;
Land and sea
Give themselves up to jollity,
And with the heart of May
Doth every Beast keep holiday ;—
Thou Child of Joy,
Shout round me, let me hear thy shouts, thou happy
Shepherd-boy !

Ye blessèd Creatures, I have heard the call
Ye to each other make ; I see
The heavens laugh with you in your jubilee ;
My heart is at your festival,
My head hath its coronal,
The fulness of your bliss, I feel—I feel it all.
Oh evil day ! if I were sullen
While Earth herself is adorning,
This sweet May-morning,
And the Children are culling
On every side,

In a thousand valleys far and wide,
    Fresh flowers ; while the sun shines warm,
And the Babe leaps up on his Mother's arm :—
    I hear, I hear, with joy I hear !
    —But there's a Tree, of many, one,
A single Field which I have looked upon,
Both of them speak of something that is gone :
    The Pansy at my feet
    Doth the same tale repeat :
Whither is fled the visionary gleam ?
Where is it now, the glory and the dream ?

Our birth is but a sleep and a forgetting :
The Soul that rises with us, our life's Star,
    Hath had elsewhere its setting,
        And cometh from afar :
    Not in entire forgetfulness,
    And not in utter nakedness,
But trailing clouds of glory do we come
    From God, who is our home :
Heaven lies about us in our infancy !
Shades of the prison-house begin to close
    Upon the growing Boy,
But He beholds the light, and whence it flows,
    He sees it in his joy ;
The Youth, who daily farther from the east
    Must travel, still is Nature's Priest,
    And by the vision splendid
    Is on his way attended ;
At length the Man perceives it die away,
And fade into the light of common day.

Earth fills her lap with pleasures of her own ;
Yearnings she hath in her own natural kind,

And, even with something of a Mother's mind,
    And no unworthy aim,
    The homely Nurse doth all she can
To make her Foster-child, her Inmate Man,
    Forget the glories he hath known,
And that imperial palace whence he came.

Behold the Child among his new-born blisses,[1]
A six years' Darling of a pigmy size !
See, where 'mid work of his own hand he lies,
Fretted by sallies of his mother's kisses,
With light upon him from his father's eyes !
See, at his feet, some little plan or chart,
Some fragment from his dream of human life,
Shaped by himself with newly-learned art ;
    A wedding or a festival,
    A mourning or a funeral ;
        And this hath now his heart,
    And unto this he frames his song :
        Then will he fit his tongue
To dialogues of business, love, or strife ;
    But it will not be long
    Ere this be thrown aside,
    And with new joy and pride
The little Actor cons another part ;
Filling from time to time his " humorous stage "
With all the Persons, down to palsied Age,
That Life brings with her in her equipage ;
    As if his whole vocation
    Were endless imitation.

Thou, whose exterior semblance doth belie
    Thy Soul's immensity ;
Thou best Philosopher, who yet dost keep

---

1 The reference is to Coleridge's little son, Hartley.

WORDSWORTH & HIS POETRY

Thy heritage, thou Eye among the blind,
That, deaf and silent, read'st the eternal deep,
Haunted for ever by the eternal mind,—
    Mighty Prophet ! Seer blest !
    On whom those truths do rest,
Which we are toiling all our lives to find,
In darkness lost, the darkness of the grave ;
Thou, over whom thy Immortality
Broods like the Day, a Master o'er a Slave,
A Presence which is not to be put by ;
Thou little Child, yet glorious in the might
Of heaven-born freedom on thy being's height,
Why with such earnest pains dost thou provoke
The years to bring the inevitable yoke,
Thus blindly with thy blessedness at strife ?
Full soon thy Soul shall have her earthly freight,
And custom lie upon thee with a weight,
Heavy as frost, and deep almost as life !

    O joy ! that in our embers
    Is something that doth live,
    That nature yet remembers
    What was so fugitive !
The thought of our past years in me doth breed
Perpetual benediction : not indeed
For that which is most worthy to be blest—
Delight and liberty, the simple creed
Of Childhood, whether busy or at rest,
With new-fledged hope still fluttering in his breast :—
    Not for these I raise
    The song of thanks and praise ;
    But for those obstinate questionings
    Of sense and outward things,
    Fallings from us, vanishings ;
    Blank misgivings of a Creature
150

Moving about in worlds not realised,
High instincts before which our mortal Nature
Did tremble like a guilty Thing surprised :
  But for those first affections,
  Those shadowy recollections,
 Which, be they what they may,
Are yet the fountain light of all our day,
Are yet a master light of all our seeing ;
 Uphold us, cherish, and have power to make
Our noisy years seem moments in the being
Of the eternal Silence : truths that wake,
  To perish never ;
Which neither listlessness, nor mad endeavour,
  Nor Man nor Boy,
Nor all that is at enmity with joy,
Can utterly abolish or destroy !
  Hence in a season of calm weather
  Though inland far we be,
Our Souls have sight of that immortal sea
  Which brought us hither,
  Can in a moment travel thither,
And see the Children sport upon the shore,
And hear the mighty waters rolling evermore.

Then sing, ye Birds, sing, sing a joyous song !
  And let the young Lambs bound
  As to the tabor's sound !
We in thought will join your throng,
  Ye that pipe and ye that play,
  Ye that through your hearts to-day
  Feel the gladness of the May !
What though the radiance which was once so bright
Be now for ever taken from my sight,
  Though nothing can bring back the hour
Of splendour in the grass, of glory in the flower ;

We will grieve not, rather find
Strength in what remains behind ;
In the primal sympathy
Which having been must ever be ;
In the soothing thoughts that spring
Out of human suffering ;
In the faith that looks through death,
In years that bring the philosophic mind.

And O, ye Fountains, Meadows, Hills, and Groves,
Forebode not any severing of our loves !
Yet in my heart of hearts I feel your might ;
I only have relinquished one delight
To live beneath your more habitual sway.
I love the Brooks which down their channels fret,
Even more than when I tripped lightly as they ;
The innocent brightness of a new-born Day
        Is lovely yet ;
The Clouds that gather round the setting sun
Do take a sober colouring from an eye
That hath kept watch o'er man's mortality ;
Another race hath been, and other palms are won.
Thanks to the human heart by which we live,
Thanks to its tenderness, its joys, and fears,
To me the meanest flower that blows can give
Thoughts that do often lie too deep for tears.

XII

A SECOND child, a girl christened Dorothy, had been born in August 1804, and when in June 1805 a third child, Thomas, came, Dove Cottage was found to be too small for the fast increasing family. The Wordsworths were therefore compelled to leave

152

it, and while seeking another home of their own to suit them, spent the winter of 1806–7 in a farmhouse at Coleorton, Leicestershire, lent to them by Sir George Beaumont.   Here they were visited by Coleridge, on his return from Malta, to whom Wordsworth read the now finished "Prelude."   Then in the follcwing summer they took a newly built house, Allan Bank, on the height between Grasmere and Easedale. Here they had to encounter all the discomforts of damp cellars and smoky chimneys ; on one cold day, it is recorded, the whole family had to go to bed because not a fire in the house could be induced to burn.   The worst of these defects were, however, remedied, and the Wordsworths remained at Allan Bank till the spring of 1811. There Coleridge, broken in health and in wretched spirits, was again their guest ; there they were also visited by De Quincey, who presently became the tenant of Dove Cottage ; and there two more children were born, Catherine in 1808 and William in 1810. Another migration was then made, this time to Grasmere Parsonage. But the death of two of the children, Catherine in her fourth year and Thomas in his seventh, made the house un-bearable to the sorrowing father.   "It stands close to the churchyard," he wrote to Lord Lonsdale, "and I have found it absolutely necessary that we should quit a place which, by recalling to our minds at every moment the losses we have sustained in the course of the last year, would grievously retard our progress towards that tranquillity which it is our duty to aim at.'' In the spring of 1813 Wordsworth accordingly left the parsonage and settled at Rydal Mount, which was to be his home for the rest of his life.

While at Coleorton he was busy chiefly with the preparation of the two volumes of his works which appeared in 1807. Among the new poems in these volumes was the '' Song at the Feast of Brougham Castle,'' which is specially remarkable for the closing stanzas describing '' the good Lord Clifford.'' The second of these might fittingly be applied to the poet himself :

Alas ! the impassioned minstrel did not know
How, by Heaven's grace, this Clifford's heart was
    framed,
How he, long forced in humble walks to go,
Was softened into feeling, soothed, and tamed.

Love had he found in huts where poor men lie ;
His daily teachers had been woods and rills,
The silence that is in the starry sky,
The sleep that is among the lonely hills.

In him the savage virtue of the Race,
Revenge, and all ferocious thoughts were dead :
Nor did he change ; but kept in lofty place
The wisdom which adversity had bred.

Glad were the vales, and every cottage hearth ;
The Shepherd-lord was honoured more and more ;
And, ages after he was laid in earth,
'' The good Lord Clifford '' was the name he bore.

154

These fine stanzas contain, in Dowden's phrase, the "peculiar virtue" of the poem. But as the same critic notes, its "feudal and chivalric spirit" is also very striking. That spirit reappears in "The White Doe of Rylstone," founded on a local tradition connected with the country round Bolton Priory, which Wordsworth visited in the summer of the same year. In that poem, as he himself perceived, he apparently challenged comparison with Scott. There is thus some interest in his own statement of the essential difference between his work on a feudal subject and that of his great contemporary. Scott, he pointed out, had concerned himself only with external incident. He on the other hand had been preoccupied with the underlying moral and spiritual meaning of his story.

During the interval between the vacating of Dove Cottage and the settlement at Rydal Mount, Wordsworth worked hard at "The Excursion," the greater part of which was written at this time. He also came forward as a politician and prose writer on current events. The most considerable result of his industry in this field was the pamphlet on the Convention of Cintra, which Canning thought the finest piece of political eloquence which had appeared since Burke, and in which he energetically supported the rights of the Peninsular peoples against the military despotism of France. Naturally his interest in such questions overflowed into verse, and thus we have a number

of political sonnets which have often been compared with the political sonnets of Milton.
Those " composed while the author was engaged
in writing a Tract occasioned by the Convention
of Cintra " are very characteristic.

Not 'mid the world's vain objects that enslave
The free-born Soul—that World whose vaunted skill
In selfish interest perverts the will,
Whose factions lead astray the wise and brave—
Not there ; but in dark wood and rocky cave,
And hollow vale which foaming torrents fill
With omnipresent murmur as they rave
Down their steep beds, that never shall be still :
Here, mighty Nature ! in this school sublime
I weigh the hopes and fears of suffering Spain ;
For her consult the auguries of time,
And through the human heart explore my way ;
And look and listen—gathering, whence I may,
Triumph, and thoughts no bondage can restrain.

Alas ! what boots the long laborious quest
Of moral prudence, sought through good and ill ;
Or pains abstruse—to elevate the will,
And lead us on to that transcendent rest
Where every passion shall the sway attest
Of Reason, seated on her sovereign hill ;
What is it but a vain and curious skill,
If sapient Germany must lie deprest,
Beneath the brutal sword ?—Her haughty Schools
Shall blush ; and may not we with sorrow say—
A few strong instincts and a few plain rules,
Among the herdsmen of the Alps, have wrought
More for mankind at this unhappy day
Than all the pride of intellect and thought ?

WORDSWORTH & HIS POETRY

The mention of Milton above will excuse the introduction here of another sonnet, also born of political interests, though dating from some years earlier.

> Milton ! thou should'st be living at this hour :
> England hath need of thee : she is a fen
> Of stagnant waters : altar, sword, and pen,
> Fireside, the heroic wealth of hall and bower,
> Have forfeited their ancient English dower
> Of inward happiness.   We are selfish men ;
> Oh ! raise us up, return to us again ;
> And give us manners, virtue, freedom, power.
> Thy soul was like a Star, and dwelt apart :
> Thou hadst a voice whose sound was like the sea :
> Pure as the naked heavens, majestic, free,
> So didst thou travel on life's common way,
> In cheerful godliness ; and yet thy heart
> The lowliest duties on herself did lay.

XIII

RYDAL MOUNT stands on the sloping side of a rocky hill called Nab Scar. Below are Rydal Lake and the Rothay, flowing down to Windermere ; in front, " a length of level valley, the extended lake, and a terminating ridge of low hills " ; behind and on both sides, " lofty fells which," Wordsworth noticed, brought " the heavenly bodies to touch, as it were, the earth upon the mountain tops," while among the valleys they seemed to shine " as winter lamps at a distance among the leafless trees." These observations led him,

soon after his settlement at the Mount, to write
the following verses :

If thou indeed derive thy light from Heaven,
Then, to the measure of that heaven-born light,
Shine, Poet ! in thy place, and be content :—
The stars pre-eminent in magnitude,
And they that from the zenith dart their beams,
(Visible though they be to half the earth,
Though half a sphere be conscious of their brightness)
Are yet of no diviner origin,
No purer essence, than the one that burns,
Like an untended watch-fire on the ridge
Of some dark mountain ; or than those which seem
Humbly to hang, like twinkling winter lamps,
Among the branches of the leafless trees.
All are the undying offspring of one Sire :
Then, to the measure of the light vouchsafed,
Shine, Poet ! in thy place, and be content.

Wordsworth's appointment, at Lord Lonsdale's instigation, as distributor of stamps for
Westmorland at a salary of £400 a year made
a welcome addition to his resources at a time
when they were being rather sorely taxed by
the needs of his fast growing family. He now
gave much time to the education of his eldest
son, and this led him to a careful re-reading of
some of the Latin writers, notably Vergil, a poet
whose spirit was in many ways cognate with his
own. A new inspiration—that of classic story
—thus came into his work, the most important
result of which is the fine poem " Laodamia."
When the remarkable chasteness of diction in

this poem is carefully considered, no surprise
will be felt at Wordsworth's assertion that it
cost him more trouble than " almost anything
of equal length " he had ever written.

LAODAMIA

" With sacrifice before the rising morn
Vows have I made by fruitless hope inspired ;
And from the infernal Gods, 'mid shades forlorn
Of night, my slaughtered Lord have I required :
Celestial pity I again implore ;—
Restore him to my sight—great Jove, restore ! "

So speaking, and by fervent love endowed
With faith, the Suppliant heavenward lifts her hands ;
While, like the sun emerging from a cloud,
Her countenance brightens—and her eye expands ;
Her bosom heaves and spreads, her stature grows ;
And she expects the issue in repose.

O terror ! what hath she perceived ?—O joy !
What doth she look on ?—whom doth she behold ?
Her Hero slain upon the beach of Troy ?
His vital presence ? his corporeal mould ?
It is—if sense deceive her not—'tis He !
And a God leads him, wingèd Mercury !

Mild Hermes spake—and touched her with his wand
That calms all fear ; " Such grace hath crowned thy
        prayer,
Laodamía ! that at Jove's command
Thy Husband walks the paths of upper air :
He comes to tarry with thee three hours' space ;
Accept the gift, behold him face to face ! "

159

Forth sprang the impassioned Queen her Lord to clasp ;
Again that consummation she essayed ;
But unsubstantial Form eludes her grasp
As often as that eager grasp was made.
The Phantom parts—but parts to re-unite,
And re-assume his place before her sight.

" Protesiláus, lo ! thy guide is gone !
Confirm, I pray, the vision with thy voice :
This is our palace,—yonder is thy throne ;
Speak, and the floor thou tread'st on will rejoice.
Not to appal me have the gods bestowed
This precious boon ; and blest a sad abode.''

" Great Jove, Laodamía ! doth not leave
His gifts imperfect :—Spectre though I be,
I am not sent to scare thee or deceive ;
But in reward of thy fidelity.
And something also did my worth obtain ;
For fearless virtue bringeth boundless gain.

" Thou knowest, the Delphic oracle foretold
That the first Greek who touched the Trojan strand
Should die ; but me the threat could not withhold :
A generous cause a victim did demand ;
And forth I leapt upon the sandy plain ;
A self-devoted chief—by Hector slain.''

" Supreme of Heroes—bravest, noblest, best !
Thy matchless courage I bewail no more.
Which then, when tens of thousands were deprest
By doubt, propelled thee to the fatal shore ;
Thou found'st—and I forgive thee—here thou art—
A nobler counsellor than my poor heart.

160

" But thou, though capable of sternest deed,
Wert kind as resolute, and good as brave ;
And he, whose power restores thee, hath decreed
Thou should'st elude the malice of the grave :
Redundant are thy locks, thy lips as fair
As when their breath enriched Thessalian air.

" No Spectre greets me,—no vain Shadow this ;
Come, blooming Hero, place thee by my side !
Give, on this well-known couch, one nuptial kiss
To me, this day, a second time thy bride ! "
Jove frowned in heaven : the conscious Parcæ threw
Upon those roseate lips a Stygian hue.

" This visage tells thee that my doom is past :
Nor should the change be mourned, even if the joys
Of sense were able to return as fast
And surely as they vanish.   Earth destroys
Those raptures duly—Erebus disdains :
Calm pleasures there abide—majestic pains.

" Be taught, O faithful Consort, to control
Rebellious passion : for the Gods approve
The depth, and not the tumult, of the soul ;
A fervent, not ungovernable, love.
Thy transports moderate ; and meekly mourn
When I depart, for brief is my sojourn—"

" Ah, wherefore ?—Did not Hercules by force
Wrest from the guardian Monster of the tomb
Alcestis, a reanimated corse,
Given back to dwell on earth in vernal bloom ?
Medea's spells dispersed the weight of years,
And Æson stood a youth 'mid youthful peers.

WORDSWORTH & HIS POETRY

" The Gods to us are merciful—and they
Yet further may relent : for mightier far
Than strength of nerve and sinew, or the sway
Of magic potent over sun and star,
Is love, though oft to agony distrest,
And though his favourite seat be feeble woman's
     breast.

" But if thou goest, I follow—" " Peace ! " he said,—
She looked upon him and was calmed and cheered ;
The ghastly colour from his lips had fled ;
In his deportment, shape, and mien, appeared
Elysian beauty, melancholy grace,
Brought from a pensive though a happy place.

He spake of love. such love as Spirits feel
In worlds whose course is equable and pure ;
No fears to beat away—no strife to heal—
The past unsighed for, and the future sure ;
Spake of heroic arts in graver mood
Revived, with finer harmony pursued ;

Of all that is most beauteous—imaged there
In happier beauty ; more pellucid streams,
An ampler ether, a diviner air,
And fields invested with purpureal gleams ;
Climes which the sun, who sheds the brightest day
Earth knows, is all unworthy to survey.

Yet there the Soul shall enter which hath earned
That privilege by virtue.—" Ill," said he,
" The end of man's existence I discerned,
Who from ignoble games and revelry
Could draw, when we had parted, vain delight,
While tears were thy best pastime, day and night ;
162

WORDSWORTH & HIS POETRY

" And while my youthful peers before my eyes
(Each hero following his peculiar bent)
Prepared themselves for glorious enterprise
By martial sports,—or, seated in the tent,
Chieftains and kings in council were detained ;
What time the fleet at Aulis lay enchained.

" The wished-for wind was given :—I then revolved
The oracle, upon the silent sea ;
And, if no worthier led the way, resolved
That, of a thousand vessels, mine should be
The foremost prow in pressing to the strand,—
Mine the first blood that tinged the Trojan sand.

" Yet bitter, oft-times bitter, was the pang
When of thy loss I thought, belovèd Wife !
On thee too fondly did my memory hang,
And on the joys we shared in mortal life,—
The paths which we had trod—these fountains, flowers,
My new-planned cities, and unfinished towers.

" But should suspense permit the Foe to cry,
' Behold they tremble !—haughty their array,
Yet of their number no one dares to die ? '
In soul I swept the indignity away :
Old frailties then recurred :—but lofty thought,
In act embodied, my deliverance wrought.

" And Thou, though strong in love, art all too weak
In reason, in self-government too slow ;
I counsel thee by fortitude to seek
Our blest re-union in the shades below.
The invisible world with thee hath sympathised ;
Be thy affections raised and solemnised.

163

" Learn, by a mortal yearning, to ascend—
Seeking a higher object.   Love was given,
Encouraged, sanctioned, chiefly for that end ;
For this the passion to excess was driven—
That self might be annulled : her bondage prove
The fetters of a dream, opposed to love."—

Aloud she shrieked ! for Hermes reappears !
Round the dear Shade she would have clung—'tis
    vain :
The hours are past—too brief had they been years ;
And him no mortal effort can detain :
Swift, toward the realms that know not earthly day,
He through the portal takes his silent way,
And on the palace-floor a lifeless corse She lay.

Thus, all in vain exhorted and reproved,
She perished ; and, as for a wilful crime,
By the just Gods whom no weak pity moved,
Was doomed to wear out her appointed time,
Apart from happy Ghosts, that gather flowers
Of blissful quiet 'mid unfading bowers.

—Yet tears to human suffering are due ;
And mortal hopes defeated and o'erthrown
Are mourned by man, and not by man alone,
As fondly he believes.—Upon the side
Of Hellespont (such faith was entertained)
A knot of spiry trees for ages grew
From out the tomb of him for whom she died ;
And ever, when such stature they had gained
That Ilium's walls were subject to their view,
The trees' tall summits withered at the sight ;
A constant interchange of growth and blight !

WORDSWORTH & HIS POETRY

This poem was written in 1814. In the autumn of that year, in company with his wife and sister-in-law Sarah Hutchinson, Wordsworth made a second tour in Scotland. Ten years before he and Dorothy had been on the point of visiting the Yarrow, so famous in the history and romance of the Border, but had after all decided to reserve the pleasure for some future occasion. This had been the theme of " Yarrow Unvisited " :

> Let beeves and home-bred kine partake
> The sweets of Burn-mill meadow ;
> The swan on still St. Mary's Lake
> Float double, swan and shadow !
> We will not see them ; will not go,
> To-day, nor yet to-morrow,
> Enough if in our hearts we know
> There's such a place as Yarrow.
>
> Be Yarrow stream unseen, unknown !
> It must, or we shall rue it :
> We have a vision of our own ;
> Ah ! why should we undo it ?
> The treasured dreams of times long past,
> We'll keep them, winsome Marrow !
> For when we're there, although 'tis fair,
> 'Twill be another Yarrow !

This time the deferred pleasure was enjoyed under the guidance of James Hogg, " the Ettrick Shepherd," and " Yarrow Visited " contains a vivid description of the poet's impressions.

165

And is this—Yarrow ?—*This* the Stream
Of which my fancy cherished,
So faithfully, a waking dream ?
An image that hath perished !
O that some Minstrel's harp were near,
To utter notes of gladness,
And chase this silence from the air,
That fills my heart with sadness ! . . .

The vapours linger round the Heights,
They melt, and soon must vanish ;
One hour is theirs, nor more is mine—
Sad thought, which I would banish,
But that I know, where'er I go,
Thy genuine image, Yarrow !
Will dwell with me—to heighten joy,
And cheer my mind in sorrow.

This year " The Excursion " was published, and the year following, the first collective edition of Wordsworth's poems, with a further essay setting out his theories of poetry. His " Thanksgiving Ode," written for the General Thanksgiving of January 1816, was his next important production. This last of any importance of his political poems, like several of the earlier sonnets, will always be noteworthy for its treatment of the character of Napoleon, in whom Wordsworth had seen from the first the incarnation of materialism, and whose downfall he welcomed as the providential vindication of spiritual forces against the " big battalions " theory for which the mighty conqueror had stood. In such protest against the mere " idolatry of power," Wordsworth was true to all the noblest ideals of his poetic vocation. None the less, as Lord Morley has said, " Waterloo may be taken for the date at which his social grasp began to fail." By this time he had travelled far from the political faith of his young manhood ; he was now a tory among the tories ; and henceforth the march of events in England only served to make him the more narrow and obstinate in his toryism. Hence we find him, in his extreme reaction against the movements which in his youth had shaken the framework of society, zealously supporting existing institutions and even the abuses which presently inspired a fresh energy of reform. He saw in " the feudal power yet surviving in England " a bulwark against the growth of that popular government which he had come to dread. He allied himself with the forces of intolerance and obscurantism. He opposed Catholic Emancipation and the Reform Bill, and wrote a sonnet attacking the Ballot. He was justified indeed in seeing spiritual power at work in Napoleon's overthrow. But it is deplorable that his theory of the divine government of the world should lead him to suggest that the cholera was God's condemnation of the great reforms which he loathed.

These things, however, do not in themselves much concern us here. It is more to the point to remember that, as Lord Morley further says, Wordsworth's " poetic glow " began to fail along with his " social grasp." We are now entering upon the long period of his decline. For thirty years more he continued to write with all the old industry and with occasional visitations of the old fire. But he added little of vital importance to the work which he had done. Indeed, we may almost say, with the critic just quoted, that in the following great poem of 1818 we have " our last glimpse of Wordsworth in the full and peculiar power of his genius."

COMPOSED UPON AN EVENING OF EXTRAORDINARY SPLENDOUR AND BEAUTY

Had this effulgence disappeared
With flying haste, I might have sent,
Among the speechless clouds, a look
Of blank astonishment ;
But 'tis endued with power to stay,
And sanctify one closing day,
That frail Mortality may see—
What is ?—ah no, but what *can* be !
Time was when field and watery cove
With modulated echoes rang,
While choirs of fervent Angels sang
Their vespers in the grove ;
Or, crowning, star-like, each some sovereign height,
Warbled, for heaven above and earth below,
Strains suitable to both.—Such holy rite,
Methinks, if audibly repeated now
From hill or valley, could not move
Sublimer transport, purer love,

Than doth this silent spectacle—the gleam—
The shadow—and the peace supreme !

No sound is uttered,—but a deep
And solemn harmony pervades
The hollow vale from steep to steep,
And penetrates the glades.
Far-distant images draw nigh,
Called forth by wondrous potency
Of beamy radiance, that imbues,
Whate'er it strikes, with gem-like hues !
In vision exquisitely clear,
Herds range along the mountain side ;
And glistening antlers are descried ;
And gilded flocks appear.
Thine is the tranquil hour, purpureal Eve !
But long as god-like wish, or hope divine,
Informs my spirit, ne'er can I believe
That this magnificence is wholly thine !
—From worlds not quickened by the sun
A portion of the gift is won ;
An intermingling of Heaven's pomp is spread
On ground which British shepherds tread !

And, if there be whom broken ties
Afflict, or injuries assail,
Yon hazy ridges to their eyes
Present a glorious scale,
Climbing suffused with sunny air,
To stop—no record hath told where !
And tempting Fancy to ascend,
And with immortal Spirits blend !
—Wings at my shoulders seem to play ;
But, rooted here, I stand and gaze
On those bright steps that heavenward raise

Their practicable way.
Come forth, ye drooping old men, look abroad,
And see to what fair countries ye are bound !
And if some traveller, weary of his road,
Hath slept since noon-tide on the grassy ground,
Ye Genii ! to his covert speed ;
And wake him with such gentle heed
As may attune his soul to meet the dower
Bestowed on this transcendent hour !

Such hues from their celestial Urn
Were wont to stream before mine eye,
Where'er it wandered in the morn
Of blissful infancy.
This glimpse of glory, why renewed ?
Nay, rather speak with gratitude ;
For, if a vestige of those gleams
Survived, 'twas only in my dreams.
Dread Power ! whom peace and calmness serve
No less than Nature's threatening voice,
If aught unworthy be my choice,
From THEE if I would swerve ;
Oh, let thy grace remind me of the light
Full early lost, and fruitlessly deplored ;
Which, at this moment, on my waking sight
Appears to shine, by miracle restored ;
My soul, though yet confined to earth,
Rejoices in a second birth !
—'Tis past, the visionary splendour fades ;
And night approaches with her shades.[1]

In 1820 Wordsworth spent four months
abroad with his wife, Dorothy, and some friends,

[1] " Allusions to the Ode entitled ' Intimations of Immortality,' " Wordsworth pointed out, " pervade the last stanza of the foregoing Poem."

WORDSWORTH & HIS POETRY

and recorded his impressions in a number of
sonnets and brief poems which he published as
" Memorials of a Tour on the Continent."
That year he also published " The River
Duddon : A Series of Sonnets," in several of
which there is a welcome return of the old
power and felicity. The two examples here
given are the 18th and the 34th.

SEATHWAITE CHAPEL

Sacred Religion ! " mother of form and fear,"
Dread arbitress of mutable respect,
New rites ordaining when the old are wrecked,
Or cease to please the fickle worshipper ;
Mother of Love ! (that name best suits thee here)
Mother of Love ! for this deep vale, protect
Truth's holy lamp, pure source of bright effect,
Gifted to purge the vapoury atmosphere
That seeks to stifle it ;—as in those days
When this low Pile a Gospel Teacher knew,
Whose good works formed an endless retinue :
A Pastor such as Chaucer's verse portrays ;
Such as the heaven-taught skill of Herbert drew ;
And tender Goldsmith crowned with deathless
    praise !

AFTER-THOUGHT

I thought of Thee, my partner and my guide,
As being past away.—Vain sympathies !
For, backward, Duddon, as I cast my eyes,
I see what was, and is, and will abide ;

171

Still glides the Stream, and shall for ever glide ;
The Form remains, the Function never dies ;
While we, the brave, the mighty, and the wise,
We Men, who in our morn of youth defied
The elements, must vanish ;—be it so !
Enough, if something from our hands have power
To live, and act, and serve the future hour ;
And if, as toward the silent tomb we go,
Through love, through hope, and faith's transcendent
    dower,
We feel that we are greater than we know.

Another and more ambitious series, which appeared in 1822, was that of the " Ecclesiastical Sonnets," to which reference has already been made. The chief influence behind these is to be found in the conversations on church history which, while a guest at Coleorton, Wordsworth had with Beaumont, who was then building a new church on his estate, though popular interest in the Catholic Relief Bill, then under discussion, doubtless acted as a further stimulus. In them Wordsworth undertakes to trace the history of the Church in England from the introduction of Christianity into Britain down to his own times. Their title is well chosen, for they are ecclesiastical poems in the narrower sense of the term, and not, except in a secondary way, religious or devotional. That in these sonnets he should have anticipated at various points the ideas of the Oxford Movement of some years later, especially in his defence of Laud, is certainly a fact upon which passing emphasis may be laid.

Yet his Anglicanism did not prevent him from
sympathizing with the leaders of the Reforma-
tion, nor did it destroy his old admiration of
Milton, greatly as he regretted "some of his
opinions, whether theological or political." [1]
I select for transcription the opening sonnet of
Part iii, which is remarkable at least for the
circumstances of its composition. It was,
Wordsworth relates, the result of a dream ; the
figure seen was that of his daughter ; the
"whole passed as here represented" ; and the
poem was conceived and completed "word for
word as it now stands" in the course of a
walk from Grasmere to Ambleside. It was
not often, Wordsworth adds, that his sonnets
were thus produced in a finished state by
such a single effort. "Most of them," on
the contrary, "were frequently retouched in
the course of composition, and, not a few,
laboriously."

I saw the figure of a lovely Maid
Seated alone beneath a darksome tree,
Whose fondly-overhanging canopy
Set off her brightness with a pleasing shade.
No Spirit was she ; *that* my heart betrayed,
For she was one I loved exceedingly ;
But while I gazed in tender reverie
(Or was it sleep that with my Fancy played ?)
The bright corporeal presence—form and face—
Remaining still distinct grew thin and rare,
Like sunny mist ;—at length the golden hair,

[1] Note to "At Vallombrosa," in "Memorials of a Tour in Italy."

> Shape, limbs, and heavenly features, keeping pace
> Each with the other in a lingering race
> Of dissolution, melted into air.

Happy as he was at home, Wordsworth continued to feel that yearning for travel which, as he confessed, was ingrained in his character. In 1823 he was again abroad, this time with his wife as his only companion. In 1824 he took his wife and daughter to North Wales, visiting his old friend Jones, with whom he had made his first memorable expedition many years before. In 1825 there was much talk in the household of a long residence on the Continent. This came to nothing at the time. But when in 1827 Sir George Beaumont died, leaving to Wordsworth an annuity of £100 to be spent in a yearly tour, the plan which had been dropped was taken up again, though in a less ambitious form, and in 1828 he started with his daughter and Coleridge for Belgium and the Rhine. Then in 1831 came his third visit to Scotland, during which he again and for the last time saw Scott, then hopelessly shattered in health and on the eve of that visit to the Continent from which he was to return only to die. This sad meeting was the theme of the third Yarrow poem.

YARROW REVISITED

> The gallant Youth, who may have gained,
>   Or seeks, a " winsome Marrow,"
> Was but an Infant in the lap
>   When first I looked on Yarrow ;

WORDSWORTH & HIS POETRY

Once more, by Newark's Castle-gate
   Long left without a warder,
I stood, looked, listened, and with Thee,
   Great Minstrel of the Border !

Grave thoughts ruled wide on that sweet day,
   Their dignity installing
In gentle bosoms, while sere leaves
   Were on the bough, or falling ;
But breezes played, and sunshine gleamed—
   The forest to embolden ;
Reddened the fiery hues, and shot
   Transparence through the golden.

For busy thoughts the Stream flowed on
   In foamy agitation ;
And slept in many a crystal pool
   For quiet contemplation :
No public and no private care
   The freeborn mind enthralling,
We made a day of happy hours,
   Our happy days recalling.

Brisk Youth appeared, the Morn of youth,
   With freaks of graceful folly,—
Life's temperate Noon, her sober Eve,
   Her Night not melancholy ;
Past, present, future, all appeared
   In harmony united,
Like guests that meet, and some from far,
   By cordial love invited.

And if, as Yarrow, through the woods
   And down the meadow ranging,
Did meet us with unaltered face,
   Though we were changed and changing ;

If, *then*, some natural shadows spread
    Our inward prospect over,
The soul's deep valley was not slow
    Its brightness to recover.

Eternal blessings on the Muse,
    And her divine employment !
The blameless Muse, who trains her Sons
    For hope and calm enjoyment ;
Albeit sickness, lingering yet,
    Has o'er their pillow brooded ;
And Care waylays their steps—a Sprite
    Not easily eluded.

For thee, O Scott ! compelled to change
    Green Eildon-hill and Cheviot
For warm Vesuvio's vine-clad slopes ;
    And leave thy Tweed and Tiviot
For mild Sorento's breezy waves ;
    May classic Fancy, linking
With native Fancy her fresh aid,
    Preserve thy heart from sinking !

Oh ! while they minister to thee,
    Each vying with the other,
May Health return to mellow Age
    With Strength, her venturous brother ;
And Tiber, and each brook and rill
    Renowned in song and story,
With unimagined beauty shine,
    Nor lose one ray of glory !

For Thou, upon a hundred streams,
    By tales of love and sorrow,
Of faithful love, undaunted truth,
    Hast shed the power of Yarrow ;

176

And streams unknown, hills yet unseen,
    Wherever they invite Thee,
At parent Nature's grateful call,
    With gladness must requite Thee.

A gracious welcome shall be thine,
    Such looks of love and honour
As thy own Yarrow gave to me
    When first I gazed upon her ;
Beheld what I had feared to see,
    Unwilling to surrender
Dreams treasured up from early days,
    The holy and the tender.

And what, for this frail world, were all
    That mortals do or suffer,
Did no responsive harp, no pen,
    Memorial tribute offer ?
Yea, what were mighty Nature's self ?
    Her features, could they win us,
Unhelped by the poetic voice
    That hourly speaks within us ?

Nor deem that localised Romance
    Plays false with our affections ;
Unsanctifies our tears—made sport
    For fanciful dejections :
Ah, no ! the visions of the past
    Sustain the heart in feeling
Life as she is—our changeful Life,
    With friends and kindred dealing.

Bear witness, Ye, whose thoughts that day
    In Yarrow's groves were centred ;
Who through the silent portal arch
    Of mouldering Newark entered ;

And clomb the winding stair that once
   Too timidly was mounted
By the " last Minstrel," (not the last !)
   Ere he his Tale recounted.

Flow on for ever, Yarrow Stream !
   Fulfil thy pensive duty,
Well pleased that future Bards should chant
   For simple hearts thy beauty ;
To dream-light dear while yet unseen,
   Dear to the common sunshine,
And dearer still, as now I feel,
   To memory's shadowy moonshine !

Before leaving Abbotsford Wordsworth expressed the hope, which he could scarcely have felt, that Scott's health would be greatly benefited by his tour. The incident and Scott's reply were recorded by Wordsworth six years later in his " Musings near Aquapendente " :

Years followed years, and when, upon the eve
Of his last going from Tweed-side, thought turned,
Or by another's sympathy was led,
To this bright land, Hope was for him no friend,
Knowledge no help ; Imagination shaped
No promise.   Still, in more than ear-deep seats,
Survives for me, and cannot but survive
The tone of voice which wedded borrowed words
To sadness not their own, when, with faint smile
Forced by intent to take from speech its edge,
He said, " When I am there, although 'tis fair,
'Twill be another Yarrow."

Meanwhile sorrows were coming fast upon him. In the winter of 1828–29 his beloved sister was prostrated by the first serious illness

178

of her life ; her mind as well as her physical strength soon began to fail ; and before long she was a confirmed invalid. Coleridge, the " friend of more than thirty years," died in 1834. In 1836 Sarah Hutchinson, long a member of the Rydal Mount household, passed away, leaving a gap which no one else could fill. The circle of his literary acquaintances was also being rapidly thinned ; and when in 1835 came news of the death of the Ettrick Shepherd, he poured forth his sadness over his many losses in some verses of touching tenderness and simplicity. These verses show that he was beginning to experience that sense of loneliness which comes to those who, as age creeps on, find themselves the survivors of their generation, and, like Tennyson's Bedivere, " among new men, strange faces, other minds." The references, as will be seen, are to Hogg himself, Scott, Coleridge, Lamb (on whom Wordsworth had already written a memorial poem), Crabbe, and Felicia Hemans.

EXTEMPORE EFFUSION UPON THE DEATH OF JAMES HOGG

When first, descending from the moorlands,
I saw the Stream of Yarrow glide
Along a bare and open valley,
The Ettrick Shepherd was my guide.

When last along its banks I wandered,
Through groves that had begun to shed
Their golden leaves upon the pathways,
My steps the Border-minstrel led.

179

WORDSWORTH & HIS POETRY

The mighty Minstrel breathes no longer,
'Mid mouldering ruins low he lies ;
And death upon the braes of Yarrow,
Has closed the Shepherd-poet's eyes :

Nor has the rolling year twice measured,
From sign to sign, its stedfast course,
Since every mortal power of Coleridge
Was frozen at its marvellous source ;

The rapt One, of the godlike forehead,
The heaven-eyed creature sleeps in earth :
And Lamb, the frolic and the gentle,
Has vanished from his lonely hearth.

Like clouds that rake the mountain-summits,
Or waves that own no curbing hand,
How fast has brother followed brother
From sunshine to the sunless land !

Yet I, whose lids from infant slumber
Were earlier raised, remain to hear
A timid voice, that asks in whispers,
" Who next will drop and disappear ? "

Our haughty life is crowned with darkness,
Like London with its own black wreath,
On which with thee, O Crabbe ! forth-looking,
I gazed from Hampstead's breezy heath.

As if but yesterday departed,
Thou too art gone before ; but why,
O'er ripe fruit, seasonably gathered,
Should frail survivors heave a sigh ?

Mourn rather for that holy Spirit,
Sweet as the spring, as ocean deep ;
For Her who, ere her summer faded,
Has sunk into a breathless sleep.

No more of old romantic sorrows,
For slaughtered Youth or love-lorn Maid !
With sharper grief is Yarrow smitten,
And Ettrick mourns with her their Poet dead.

In 1837 Wordsworth made his last foreign
trip, to Italy. A visit to Italy had been a dream
of Dorothy's life, but she was now unable to
travel, and his friend, Crabb Robinson, was the
poet's only companion. To that friend, whose
" buoyant spirit " cheered him on his way, he
dedicated his " Memorials of a Tour in Italy."
But, as Robinson records in his " Diary," he
wrote but little, while in what he did write
" meditation predominates over observation."
This tendency of the mind to turn upon itself,
even in the midst of novelties, is evidence of
failing interest in outward things ; and Wordsworth himself felt its import. " It is too late,"
he often said on the journey ; and once : " I
have matter for volumes, had I but youth to
work it up." The ageing poet was at length
becoming aware of waning powers. One poem
among these " Memorials " possesses in his
own phrase a " rather melancholy " interest.
It is entitled " The Cuckoo at Laverna." He
had always loved the cuckoo's voice, and years
before, at Dove Cottage, he had written some
delightful verses to his favourite bird.

TO THE CUCKOO

O blithe New-comer ! I have heard,
I hear thee and rejoice.
O Cuckoo ! shall I call thee Bird,
Or but a wandering Voice ?

While I am lying on the grass
Thy twofold shout I hear,
From hill to hill it seems to pass,
At once far off, and near.

Though babbling only to the Vale,
Of sunshine and of flowers,
Thou bringest unto me a tale
Of visionary hours.

Thrice welcome, darling of the Spring !
Even yet thou art to me
No bird, but an invisible thing,
A voice, a mystery ;

The same whom in my school-boy days
I listened to ; that Cry
Which made me look a thousand ways
In bush, and tree, and sky.

To seek thee did I often rove
Through woods and on the green ;
And thou wert still a hope, a love ;
Still longed for, never seen.

And I can listen to thee yet ;
Can lie upon the plain
And listen, till I do beget
That golden time again.

> O blessèd Bird ! the earth we pace
> Again appears to be
> An unsubstantial, faery place ;
> That is fit home for Thee !

Now at Laverna he has to record his inability, through growing deafness, to hear the cuckoo's beloved cry " till Mr. Robinson had twice or thrice " directed his attention to it.

> List—'twas the Cuckoo.—O with what delight
> Heard I that voice ! and catch it now, though faint,
> Far off and faint, and melting into air,
> Yet not to be mistaken. Hark again !
> Those louder cries give notice that the Bird,
> Although invisible as Echo's self,
> Is wheeling hitherward. Thanks, happy Creature,
> For this unthought-of greeting !

XIV

ONE satisfaction the years brought to Wordsworth as some compensation for the sorrows of advancing life and this sense of declining strength. He was now at last coming into his own.

More than any other great English poet he had to suffer from protracted public neglect, and, a part cause of this, from the contempt and ridicule of the official leaders of taste, notably Jeffrey. That scolding critic, who for a long time wielded an influence hardly justified by the quality of his work, had year after year pursued the poet with the bitterest and most

reckless hostility. He denounced the volumes
of 1807 as " coarse, inelegant, and infantine " ;
described the themes of the poems as " low,
silly, and uninteresting " ; and sneered at the
verses " To the Small Celandine " as " namby-
pamby." The Immortality Ode he dismissed
as " illegible and unintelligible." Of " Alice
Fell " he wrote : " If the printing of such trash
as this be not felt as an insult to the public
taste, we are afraid that it cannot be insulted."
Speaking of " Resolution and Independence,"
he defied " the bitterest enemy of Mr. Wordsworth to produce anything at all parallel from
any collection of English poetry, or even from
the specimens of his friend Mr. Southey " (an
admirable example, by the way, of the econo-
mical practice known as killing two birds with
one stone). He declared that " The Excursion "
would " never do," and pronounced " The
White Doe of Rylstone " " the very worst poem
we ever saw imprinted in a quarto volume "
and the product of a mind in a state of " low
and maudlin imbecility." These are samples
of the " arch-critic's " judgment, and though
in places, as we must candidly admit, he erred
rather by virulence of language than by per-
version of opinion, the undiscriminating character of his criticism is obvious. Wordsworth
himself took these attacks with extraordinary
equanimity, and begged Lady Beaumont not to
be disturbed by them. " Never forget," he
wrote to her, in a spirit of calm self-confidence,
" what, I believe, was observed to you by
184

WORDSWORTH & HIS POETRY

Coleridge, that every great and original writer, in proportion as he is great and original, must himself create the taste by which he is to be realized." Yet, though the poet was thus able to adopt the attitude of quiet indifference, Jeffrey's incessant onslaughts had certainly much to do with the tardiness of his rise to fame.

The current, however, was now turning. Public sympathy began to come round to him, and even Jeffrey was ultimately forced to make a grudging apology for his " asperity " and " *vivacités* of expression." A new generation was arising who saw greatness and meaning in his work to which their fathers had been blind. Unmistakable signs of growing reputation and influence followed within the next few years. In 1838 he received an honorary degree from the University of Durham. In 1839, Oxford, always prone to wait till her favours can be safely bestowed, granted him a similar mark of approval. In 1840 the Queen Dowager visited him at Rydal Mount. In 1842 Sir Robert Peel placed his name on the Civil List for a pension of £300 a year. In 1843, on the death of Southey, he was made poet-laureate, and actually appeared at Court, wearing a suit which he borrowed from Rogers and which, though a rather tight fit, did well enough for the occasion. He was now indeed universally regarded as the patriarch of English letters.

Three years later he lost his last surviving brother, Christopher, the Master of Trinity

College, Cambridge, and in 1847 his only
daughter Dora, who since 1841 had been the
wife of Edward Quillinan. He had borne many
sorrows with a firm courage supported by
religious faith. But he was now old, and this
unexpected blow left him heartbroken. He did
not, however, live long to mourn his beloved
child. On March 12, 1850, while sitting on a
stone seat to watch the setting sun, he caught a
chill, and had to take to his bed. Two days
afterwards he was attacked by severe pains in
his side ; on the 20th pleurisy set in ; on the
23rd he sank peacefully into his final rest. His
mind was filled with thoughts of his daughter
even to the very end. " Is that Dora ? " he
had asked, when some one had quietly drawn
the curtains of his bed.

There was some talk of burial in Westminster
Abbey. Far more appropriately his body lies
in Grasmere Churchyard, among the hills and
the people he had loved so well.

> The old rude church, with bare, bald tower, is here ;
> Beneath its shadow high-born Rotha flows ;
> Rotha, remembering well who slumbers near,
> And with cool murmur lulling his repose—
>
> Rotha, remembering well who slumbers near.
> His hills, his lakes, his streams are with him yet.
> Surely the heart that read her own heart clear
> Nature forgets not soon : 'tis we forget.[1]

[1] William Watson : " Wordsworth's Grave."

WORDSWORTH & HIS POETRY

XV

WORDSWORTH'S personality was not altogether engaging. In his own family circle, indeed, and in his daily intercourse with his rustic neighbours he was kind and sympathetic, and, as we are told by Sir Henry Taylor and others, even in general society, where he was very much less at home, he could at times unbend and take his share of the talk about him with a certain dignified grace. But we feel that on the whole he lacked geniality and flexibility, that he was a little stiff, a little austere, often even a little pompous and not a little dull. He wanted, too, breadth of outlook, and while undoubtedly his exclusive attention to the few great subjects of his choice gave him the power which comes of concentration in his own special field, such advantage was purchased by the sacrifice of many interests which add richness and variety to human life. The absence of any sense of humour from his intellectual composition must also be recognized as another serious defect. But the feature of his character which perhaps most unfavourably impressed those who met him, at all events in his later years, was his entire engrossment with himself. By temperament he was self-centred and self-contained, and the peculiar conditions of his life—his isolation, his lonely and introspective habits, his intense preoccupation with his own work, the worship paid to him by a

187

small coterie of ardent admirers, the neglect of the general public, and the abuse of the critics— all helped in different ways to deepen his self-absorption into an egotism which was not the less to be regretted because it was bound up with some of the most estimable qualities of his nature.   One unfortunate aspect of this egotism was his inability to appreciate the work of his contemporaries in literature, even when, as in the case of Scott and Southey, for example, they happened to be personal friends.

These, however, are but the shortcomings— the negligible shortcomings—of an essentially strong and noble character ; and it is upon the strength and the nobility that I prefer here to dwell.   A north-countryman to his backbone, if he had something of the hardness he had also the sterling virtues of the stock from which he sprang.   His simplicity, his indifference to worldly honour and emolument, his steady devotion to his art and mission, are alike admirable.   Admirable, too, are his fortitude, his self-control, the stability of his mind, and his fine power of linking the ideal with the commonplaces of the everyday lot.   Like his own skylark, he was

Type of the wise who soar, but never roam,
True to the kindred points of Heaven and Home.

The " plain living and high thinking " which he inculcated were his own rule and inspiration. The purity, the lofty temper, the utter trans-

WORDSWORTH & HIS POETRY

parency of soul which we find in his poetry we find also in his life.

Let me add a pen-portrait of the poet in his old age from the hand of that great master of portraiture, Carlyle, who met him at one of Sir Henry Taylor's literary breakfast parties.

He talked well in his way, with veracity, easy brevity, and force—as a wise tradesman would of his tools and workshop, and as no unwise one could. His voice was good, frank, and sonorous, though practically clear, distinct and forcible, rather than melodious ; the tone of him business-like, sedately confident ; no discourtesy, yet no anxiety about being courteous : a fine wholesome rusticity, fresh as his mountain breezes, sat well on this stalwart veteran, and on all he said and did. You would have said he was a usually taciturn man, glad to unlock himself to audience sympathetic and intelligent when such offered itself. His face bore marks of much, not always peaceful, meditation ; the look of it not bland or benevolent, so much as close, impregnable, and hard ; a man *multa tacere loquive paratus,* in a world where he had experienced no lack of contradictions as he strode along ! The eyes were not very brilliant, but they had a quiet clearness ; there was enough of brow, and well shaped ; rather too much of cheek ("horse face" I have heard satirists say), face of squarish shape and decidedly longish, as I think the head itself was (*its* "length" going *horizontal*). He was large-boned, lean, but still firm-knit, tall, and strong-looking when he stood ; a right good old steel-grey figure, with a fine rustic simplicity and dignity about him and a veracious *strength* looking through him, which might have suited one of those old steel-grey Markgrafs . . . whom Henry the Fowler set up to ward the marches and do battle with the intrusive heathen, in a stalwart and judicious manner.

One personal peculiarity may be mentioned which has a direct interest for the student of his work. Rugged of constitution and abstemious of habit, Wordsworth was able to bear with impunity any amount of exposure and physical fatigue ; but the intensity of his excitement during composition often prostrated him completely. " I have never a pen in my hand for five minutes," he once wrote to Beaumont, " before my whole frame becomes a bundle of uneasiness ; a perspiration starts out all over me, and my chest is oppressed in a manner which I cannot describe."

In a note to one of his poems, in which he rather quaintly apologizes to his wife and sister for having so often been late for dinner and further records the irritation in one of his heels caused by wearing too tight a shoe, he tells us that " poetic excitement, when accompanied by protracted labour in composition, has throughout my life brought me more or less bodily derangement." Dorothy's journals are full of such entries as these : " William worked at the Leech Gatherer almost incessantly from morning till teatime . . . he wearied himself to death." " William did not sleep till three o'clock." " William very nervous." " William had a bad night, and was working at his poem." "We read the first part of the poem, and were delighted with it, but William afterwards got to some ugly place, and went to bed tired out." "Poor William wore himself out and me with labour."

Wordsworth's poetry may impress us as we read by its prevailing serenity. But if, in his own phrase, there is little in it of "the tumult of the soul," it was none the less the product of persistent application and great emotional strain.

It has been the aim of the foregoing pages to bring out not only the personal interest of that poetry, but also some of its enduring qualities. Only a few words of summary will now be necessary.

Wordsworth, as we have seen, owes his distinctive position in our literature in part to his wonderful power as an interpreter of nature, especially on the spiritual side. More than any other poet he brought to men "barricadoed evermore within the walls of cities" a revelation of the beauty and of the divine meaning of "this goodly Universe." To make them partakers of his own joy in the "living Presence of the Earth" was one important aspect of his conscious mission. Deeply deploring the blindness and deafness of the average man to the glories of the world about him, he believed that even a superstitious veneration of the forces of nature was better than apathy born of absorption in material things.

WORDSWORTH & HIS POETRY

The world is too much with us ; late and soon,
Getting and spending, we lay waste our powers :
Little we see in Nature that is ours ;
We have given our hearts away, a sordid boon !
The Sea that bares her bosom to the moon ;
The winds that will be howling at all hours,
And are up-gathered now like sleeping flowers ;
For this, for everything, we are out of tune ;
It moves us not.—Great God ! I'd rather be
A Pagan suckled in a creed outworn ;
So might I, standing on this pleasant lea,
Have glimpses that would make me less forlorn ;
Have sight of Proteus rising from the sea ;
Or hear old Triton blow his wreathèd horn.

It was Wordsworth's constant purpose to overcome the apathy against which he makes this passionate protest ; to open the eyes of his readers to the loveliness of nature and their souls to her divine message.

Great as an interpreter of nature, Wordsworth, however, was no less great as an interpreter of human life, and his position in this respect is equally distinctive. No one can read the poems which I have quoted without feeling this. Here again we are in touch with what I have called his conscious mission. "Every great poet is a teacher," he wrote to Beaumont. "I wish to be considered as a teacher, or as nothing." In these uncompromising words he announces his directly didactic purpose. That this purpose is often far too obtrusive in his work is of course admitted. That it is to be held responsible for the thousands

192

of lines of dull and prosy moralizings which he gives us, for instance, in " The Excursion," is equally evident. But if too often, in his capacity of mere homilist, he is satisfied with the bare inculcation of moral truth, in his really inspired moods, in his really vital verse, moral truth is transmuted by him into the purest poetry ; and then, as in the " Lines Written a Few Miles above Tintern Abbey," he is great at once as a poet and as a teacher. There is nothing, indeed, pretentious or particularly recondite about his philosophy. It deals with a few central thoughts, and these thoughts can be easily formulated and understood. But its simplicity is part of its virtue and strength. Wordsworth, in fact, is deep because he is simple. Brushing aside the merely artificial and conventional ideas about life and its values in which we are accustomed to rest, but which confuse our vision and hamper our spiritual freedom, he throws his emphasis continually upon the things which are elemental and essential—upon those primary affections and impregnable instincts which lie at the very root of life. He addresses himself to the power which we have latent within us to lift ourselves by resolute effort above the entanglements of circumstance and to live at peace within ourselves. Above all, let us remember, he is so bracing and helpful because he is the poet of happiness, and because, by proclaiming that the secret of true happiness is to be sought, not in external conditions, but in the soul, he shows us where we may purchase it " without

money and without price." Virtue, for him, is
the one road to such happiness, and happiness
is its final reward, and though, in Sir Henry
Taylor's words, he recognizes that " genial
virtue " must often fall back upon " severe
virtue for support," moral struggle and the
strenuousness of moral purpose must, he
teaches, ultimately issue in the abounding joy
which comes to a nature attuned to the demands
of eternal law.   Such is the theme of one of his
noblest poems.

ODE TO DUTY

Stern Daughter of the Voice of God !
O Duty ! if that name thou love
Who art a light to guide, a rod
To check the erring, and reprove ;
Thou, who art victory and law
When empty terrors overawe ;
From vain temptations dost set free ;
And calm'st the weary strife of frail humanity !

There are who ask not if thine eye
Be on them ; who, in love and truth,
Where no misgiving is, rely
Upon the genial sense of youth :
Glad Hearts ! without reproach or blot
Who do thy work, and know it not :
Oh ! if through confidence misplaced
They fail, thy saving arms, dread Power ! around them
    cast.

Serene will be our days and bright,
And happy will our nature be,

WORDSWORTH & HIS POETRY

When love is an unerring light,
And joy its own security.
And they a blissful course may hold
Even now, who, not unwisely bold,
Live in the spirit of this creed ;
Yet seek thy firm support, according to their need.

I, loving freedom, and untried ;
No sport of every random gust,
Yet being to myself a guide,
Too blindly have reposed my trust :
And oft, when in my heart was heard
Thy timely mandate, I deferred
The task, in smoother walks to stray ;
But thee I now would serve more strictly, if I may.

Through no disturbance of my soul,
Or strong compunction in me wrought,
I supplicate for thy control ;
But in the quietness of thought :
Me this unchartered freedom tires ;
I feel the weight of chance-desires :
My hopes no more must change their name,
I long for a repose that ever is the same.

Stern Lawgiver ! yet thou dost wear
The Godhead's most benignant grace ;
Nor know we anything so fair
As is the smile upon thy face :
Flowers laugh before thee on their beds
And fragrance in thy footing treads ;
Thou dost preserve the stars from wrong ;
And the most ancient heavens, through Thee, are
    fresh and strong.

To humbler functions, awful Power !
I call thee : I myself commend

Unto thy guidance from this hour ;
Oh, let my weakness have an end !
Give unto me, made lowly wise,
The spirit of self-sacrifice ;
The confidence of reason give ;
And in the light of truth thy Bondman let me live !

If, as Emerson finely says, " the great poets are judged by the frame of mind they induce," the greatness of the writer of these superb verses is surely beyond question.

Wordsworth's inequalities must be apparent to every one who considers his production as a whole, and must be frankly recognized. He wrote much when the poetic inspiration was upon him, and we have seen something of the splendid results. But he wrote much also when the poetic inspiration was not upon him, and hence the immense amount of absolutely perishable matter in his too voluminous work. More than most poets, therefore, he gains by judicious selection. But when the perishable matter has been rejected, what remains, though relatively small in bulk in proportion to the totality of his output, will hold its place secure among the world's possessions for ever. Sixty years have now passed since his death, and time has already justified his firm belief that his poems would " co-operate with the benign tendencies in human nature and society," and would, "in their degree, be efficacious in making men wiser, better, and happier."

BIBLIOGRAPHY

The following books and essays may be recommended for the further study of Wordsworth and his work :

TEXT : POEMS

" The Poetical Works of Wordsworth," ed. Knight (Library ed., 8 vols.).

" The Poetical Works of Wordsworth," ed. Knight (Eversley ed., 16 vols.).

" Wordsworth's Poems," ed. Dowden (Aldine ed., 7 vols.).

" The Poetical Works of Wordsworth," ed. T. Hutchinson (Oxford ed.).

" The Complete Poetical Works of Wordsworth " (with an Introduction by J. Morley). (Globe ed.) (This one-volume edition is the most convenient for the general student.)

" Wordsworth's Select Poems, chosen and edited with a Preface by Matthew Arnold " (Golden Treasury Series). (The preface is reprinted in Arnold's " Essays in Criticism," vol. ii.)

" Selections from Wordsworth," ed. Knight.

"Poems by Wordsworth, a Selection," ed. Dowden (with a long biographical and critical introduction). (Athenæum Press Series.)

TEXT : PROSE WORKS

" Wordsworth's Prose Works," ed. Grosart, 3 vols.

" Prose Works of Wordsworth," ed. Knight, 2 vols.

" Wordsworth's Literary Criticism," ed. N. C. Smith.

BIBLIOGRAPHY

BIOGRAPHY AND CRITICISM

D. Wordsworth : "Journals," ed. Knight, 2 vols.
"Recollections of a Tour in Scotland," ed. Shairp.

T. de Quincey : "Reminiscences of the English Lake Poets."

C. Wordsworth : "Memoirs of Wordsworth," 2 vols.

W. Knight : "Life of Wordsworth," 3 vols.

F. W. H. Myers : "Wordsworth" (English Men of Letters).

E. Legouis : "La Jeunesse de Wordsworth." (English translation by Matthews.)

D. W. Rannie : "Wordsworth and his Circle."

W. Raleigh : "Wordsworth."

L. Magnus : "Primer of Wordsworth."

J. C. Shairp : "On Poetic Interpretation of Nature."

S. A. Brooke : "Theology in the English Poets."

"Wordsworthiana : Papers read before the Wordsworth Society."

S. T. Coleridge : "Biographia Literaria," chaps. xiv-xx.

E. Caird : "Wordsworth" (in "Essays in Literature and Philosophy," vol. i).

R. W. Church : "Wordsworth" (in "Dante and Other Essays").

E. Dowden : "Prose Works of Wordsworth" (in "Studies in Literature").
"Text of Wordsworth's Poems" (in "Transcripts and Studies").

A. de Vere : "Wordsworth" (several essays in "Essays, chiefly on Poetry").
198

BIBLIOGRAPHY

R. H. Hutton : " Wordsworth " (in " Essays Theological and Literary ").

J. R. Lowell : " Wordsworth " (in " Among my Books ").

W. Pater : " Wordsworth " (in " Appreciations ").

L. Stephen : " Ethics of Wordsworth " (in " Hours in a Library," 3rd series).

W. Bagehot : " Wordsworth, Tennyson, and Browning " (in " Literary Studies," vol. ii).

For the " Wordsworth Country," see

" Wordsworth's Guide to the Lakes," ed. E. de Selincourt.

D. Masson : " In the Footsteps of the Poets."

H. D. Rawnsley : " Literary Associations of the English Lakes," 2 vols.

W. Knight : " Through the Wordsworth Country."

For the general literary history of Wordsworth's time, see

C. H. Herford : " The Age of Wordsworth " (in " Handbooks of English Literature ").

E. Dowden : " The French Revolution and English Literature."